God's Foreign Policy

God's Foreign Policy

*Practical Ways to Help
the World's Poor*

Miriam Adeney

REGENT COLLEGE PUBLISHING
VANCOUVER, BRITISH COLUMBIA

First published 1984 by
Wm. B. Eerdmans Publishing Co. (ISBN 0-8028-1968-0).

This edition reproduced 1998 with permission by Regent College Publishing,
an imprint of the Regent College Bookstore, 5800 University Boulevard, Vancouver B.C. V6T 2E4, Canada.

Library of Congress Cataloguing in Publication Data

ADENEY, MIRIAM.
    God's Foreign Policy/ Miriam Adeney.
        p.   cm.
    Includes bibliographical references.
    1. Christianity -- Developing countries. 2. Church and the poor.
    I. Title
BR115.U6 A268   1994

ISBN 1-57383-022-4

CONTENTS

ACKNOWLEDGMENTS

THANKS TO MY DAD, who is like a tree planted by the rivers of water, bringing forth his fruit in season.

Thanks to my Mother, who—when I came home from the hospital with my first son, ready to rest regally—handed me a stack of term papers, saying, "You have a contract. Go to it!"; who pushes me to perseverance and excellence.

Thanks to my husband, Michael, for his kingdom world-view, for asking significant questions; who wrote recently, "Reasons I want to go on living? You, God, the boys, tennis, work, the Church in China, Mt. Rainier, the Seattle Seahawks, sauerkraut on chocolate chip cookies, customers I help . . . the possibility that our children may become godly adults enlisted in the army of the King of Kings, praising him and doing battle with the forces of darkness. . . ."

Thanks to Daniel, Joel, and Michael Wilberforce Adeney for inundating me with the real physical world; for challenging me to keep the standards I expect of them; for comic relief.

Thanks to Bel and Lety Magalit for commissioning me in the fight for Christ and his kingdom.

Thanks to World Concern, Regent College, and Seattle Pacific University, where the ideas in this book were hammered out with field-workers and lay people.

Thanks to Vivian Tadeo and Susan Bertsch for being excellent mother substitutes, alternative adult role-models for my boys.

Thanks to Tim Dearborn for holding the world before my congregation as he brings us the Word of the Lord.

INTRODUCTION

I held tight to my husband Michael as we sliced through Manila on a Honda at the end of a hot day. The breeze bathed us. People in a kaleidoscopic variety of colored cottons milled beside us on the pavement. Some whistled. They thought I looked like Ingrid Bergman. Others yelled "Hi, Joe!"—their greeting to Americans ever since GI's waded ashore during World War II. Busses belched. Jeepneys jammed the lanes sideways. Weaving through the traffic, chuckling that our 50-cc. motorcycle was the fastest thing on the road, we clung together as outposts of the kingdom.

It was the early 1970's. Michael was a grad student at the University of the Philippines. I taught anthropology and did editing and writing. Together we were adjusting to a milieu in which natural and political hurricanes regularly demolished our best-planned systems.

Once, out of the one solid-glass window in our house, we watched the entire cycle of a typhoon. The distant winds flattened everything leftward. The near winds threw shacks and furniture to the right. Forty-foot aluminum roofs piled up at the wire-mesh fence three feet behind our house. Would one of those roofs slice through our cement-block shelter? Rain pounded day and night. Our books and papers curled and sprouted green mold spots. Spiders sidled in through the pipes. We listened to the radio and the wind and the rain, and played Scrabble.

During the eye of the storm, Michael raced to the store for a tank of gas for our stove (we had run out). As he zipped back, returning winds began to lift his motorcycle from the road. During the reprieve, squatters had scurried out and gathered up as many rich people's roofs as they could before rising tail winds lashed them back to shelter.

Afterwards, as we attempted to carry on our professional schedules in the interval before the next storm or riot, earthquake or fiesta, we waded through knee-deep water in the streets. The potholes were covered, deceptively. When we tried to navigate on our Honda, it lurched, sank, reared—and eventually stalled. Michael would run with it to dry off the motor, hop on, make a U-turn, and come charging past me, unable to stop. I would make a flying leap at him, and we would buck away to the upper-class women's college where I taught Philippine sociology to students who descended from chauffeured limousines to mouth Marxist slogans.

Manila: slums all around Imelda Marcos' "edifice complex," but also color, fashion, courtliness, contemporary cosmopolitan European influence, and the whiff of Chinese and Spanish civilizations, redolent of centuries of intrigue, style, and development. Here in this stormy queen city the blinders fell off my eyes, and I came to know poverty. I will not pretend that I wallowed in the poverty of the poorest of the poor, though I saw and picked my way through it sometimes. But I was baptized in the poverty of brothers and sisters as educated, as multidimensional, as complex as I. For whom a cassette recorder cost two months' salary. For whom a refrigerator was optional. For whom it was impossible to get fat. (Is that imaginable?)

Among the slightly poorer, I remember one Christian woman in a fishing village.

"I'm in pain," she grimaced one day as we threaded our way between bamboo houses.

"What's the trouble?"

"Masakit ang puson ko," she murmured. "Urinary tract infection."

"Can't you get medicine?"

"Yes, I'm saving money from our catch every day. So—in twenty-five days I'll have enough for the pills."

My sister. Subject to an indignity of pain and waiting that I would never tolerate. I have my rights. Such a baptism constituted my second conversion in the sense that Orlando Costas has used the term.[1] I may quibble about distinguishing between regeneration and conversion if Costas is going to use the latter term to describe every major change in his life, but I understand what he means. If we have really fraternized with poverty, we can't go home again.

As a teenager, I picked beans and strawberries in the fields of Oregon. I knew what it was to get sweaty and dirty. And I knew what it was to be prudent with money. But not what it was to be poor. Somehow I never saw the migrant laborers in our town as full, mature, responsible human beings. I saw them as shiftless. I never remember questioning what structural forces might contribute to their shiftlessness.

My dad is a small-town doctor who walks to work. He delivers babies, and years later, when they're grown, he delivers *their* babies. He listens to garrulous patients, and accepts pay in potatoes and eggs and firewood. He has created jobs by capitalizing farmers and fishermen who were out of work. He has shown me much of what it means to care for a community.

Yet, apart from charity cases personally known to us, if my family encountered poverty, we passed by and went on about our business. At least I did. The status quo generally did not hurt us. Not until I lived in the Philippines did the status quo hurt me.

One sociologist who studied the farmers of the northwestern United States found that these farmers perceived reality in three categories: (1) scenery; (2) machinery and other useful things; and (3) people. And, unconsciously, American farmers viewed American Indians more as scenery than as people—and Mexican laborers primarily as useful things. Foreign students in the Northwest have told me that they suffer not from malicious prejudice but from the dreadful loneliness that comes from being looked through, as if they weren't there. I suspect we categorize the poor and look through them in a similar way.

But today Americans travel. Many of us have lived overseas long enough to care for a poorer brother or sister to the point that when we return we would rather have a black-and-white TV, and send the friend money, than enjoy a color TV. We've changed. We've been converted to a deeper vision of the world and of what is important. Yet sending money is not a long-term answer. We know that. Ultimately, people have to support themselves. We are faced, then, with this question: What is our intelligent response to the poverty of brothers and sisters around the world?

This problem confronts every Christian lay person. It confronts every pastor. It confronts every mission committee as they meet around a table in a heated, well-constructed building.

Yet this is no time for sob stories. At the personal level, we're economically pinched. We have to struggle with mortgage payments. Medical bills. Gas. Bikes for the kids. College tuition. Even hamburger is $1.89 a pound. How far can you stretch a paycheck?

As for the poor, they often know how to cope in a crunch. In *Beyond Charity,* John Sommer explains,

> Studies have shown that in parts of the world where weather patterns are uncertain, social systems tend to respond to crop fluctuations with various mechanisms to insure against the consequences of that uncertainty. Consumption patterns may not fluctuate to the same extent as production. In good crop years, considerable compensatory saving may occur, whether in the form of grain, gold bracelets, or other objects of wealth; this serves as a safety valve for the bad years. Thus what might be seen by some outsiders as a disaster requiring external assistance may not be seen as a crisis at all by the local people. Furthermore, there is no world-wide consensus on what constitutes adequate caloric intake for people of varying genetic compositions. . . . The result, though still little researched, may be that relief programs respond too quickly and excessively for the good of the particular society over the long run.[2]

The poor often know how to handle difficult times. We're the ones who don't. We of the middle class are hard hit by inflation and recession.

Naturally, as Christians, we want to support the new addition to the church. We may feel the pastor deserves a raise. We want to give our due to missions. We're sorry that mothers in many countries must bury half of their children. But we can't handle many tear-jerkers right now. Besides, *can* we significantly help the poor? We can think of innumerable objections to extending a helping hand.

- Shouldn't evangelism be our priority?
- In any case, with poor countries so overpopulated, is it even possible to produce enough food for everybody?
- Don't our gifts often just enrich the rich? Don't the distributors rip off a lot of what we send? Or waste it through poor distribution?
- Aren't the very values of some cultures blocks to their becoming self-supporting?
- Shouldn't we tackle our own country's economic problems first?

- Aren't there biblical prophecies that indicate that the world has to get worse and worse before Jesus will come again?
- Doesn't economic aid foster dependence on us foreigners? Doesn't that produce "rice Christians"?
- Doesn't economic uplift make people more materialistic?

Today I am no longer trying to skirt flooded potholes on Philippine roads. I am an anthropologist. Many of my students work overseas. Some do economic development for missions. As I follow their careers, I am made keenly aware of these questions—questions about the frequent irrelevance of such development.

One of my students, a building contractor, returns home from erecting churches in Saharan Africa. A well-known Christian development agency, he tells me, has constructed a magnificent modern piggery in the south of a very poor country. But since that region is the home of animists, and the developers don't want to neglect the Muslims in the north, they built a second gleaming piggery there. Yet all those square yards of stainless steel in that northern piggery never have been used for anything except temporary housing during a smallpox epidemic—because Muslims abhor pigs.

Decisions made in the home office.

Sometimes we anthropologists don't know whether to laugh or cry as we watch such development efforts. Cross-cultural communication is difficult. If it has any effect at all, it is often disruptive. And it disrupts the good as well as the bad.

There are strengths in the Filipino lifestyle, for example, that deserve not to be diluted. My life in the Philippines was not all storms. There were idyllic days when I went snorkeling. It was another world altogether the minute I dipped my mask into the Pacific. Forests waving and bending in the current. Bold brown-and-gold-striped clownfish living symbiotically with big white sea anemones. Blue starfish. Lionfish. Eels. Sea slugs. Schools of tiny dili. Black sea urchins. The polyps of corals, big and small, undulating. In the noon heat, wonderfully cool. No wonder the Filipinos traditionally have spent so much time on and in the water. It is amazingly buoyant—and provides marvelous therapy. The fish toil not, neither spin, yet their feeding cycle progresses with stately rhythm.

Like the fish, Filipinos interact gracefully, colorfully, unhurriedly. They make hospitality an art; they love to have parties. Filipinos also interact symbiotically. No one thinks, "My apartment. My car.

My salary." Filipinos never sleep in a room alone, nor do they work or relax alone. Often I watched my landlord's grandchildren play together. Five children in one family ranged in age from one to ten. For hours they would play without any squabbles or sibling rivalry, the older ones adjusting the games to make it possible for the little ones to join in at varying levels of skill. It was expected that the older ones would take care of the younger ones. Filipino children are trained that way. Today, two of my young Filipino friends are active heads of households for several siblings and nieces and nephews. Certainly there are tensions in Philippine society, tensions increased exponentially by modernization. Nevertheless, having an apartment alone, being free from the problems of younger kin, remains unthinkable.

I shudder to see such strengths eroded by outsiders' crude efforts at economic uplift. Too often, well-intentioned development projects have weakened local social structures, eroded indigenous art, and even derailed healthful food, housing, and work habits. Too often, as with the first-class piggery in the Muslim region in Africa, our projects render us contemptible. It may be better not to meddle at all.

Yet notwithstanding the strengths of the Philippine culture, my fishing friend still must scrape together earnings for twenty-five days before she can buy the pills that will treat her infection. . . .

What, then, is our intelligent response to the poverty of such brothers and sisters?

When I lived in the Philippines it was my privilege to work on the Inter-Varsity staff with and under the direction of Filipinos who were my intellectual and spiritual superiors. Reading King James English did not come naturally to my colleagues, yet the Bible was precious. They had immersed themselves in it. They struggled to grasp each nuance of God's nature. When they prayed, they worshipped with substance.

"Thank you, Jesus, for being our rock. We don't know whether there are going to be riots at our university today—"

"And thank you for being our vine. For keeping us fresh on these hot days. We travel so long on dusty busses. Students forget to show up. . . ."

"Thank you for being our life . . . our shepherd . . . our door . . . our bread . . . our water. . . ."

Through them, I discovered new dimensions of worship.

I also discovered new dimensions of work. At the college where I taught we regularly critiqued each other's teaching—nobody was allowed to grow stale. Everyone had to write part of a book. And staff training took place on the job. Even a young woman sometimes would be sent alone to a new language area to be the lone administrator, counselor, speaker, organizer, accountant, book salesman, and correspondent—while learning the language.

In spite of scandals and disputes, the milieu was rich. Staff and students periodically formed medical teams for rural areas. Some graduates formed the Philippine Christian Lawyers' Fellowship, designed particularly to help minorities secure title to their ancestral lands. Other graduates served unselfishly in other fields. Our director, Dr. Isabelo Magalit, was a model of excellence. He and his wife Lety lived with exemplary simplicity. College-educated, Lety kept house for a husband, four children, and innumerable guests—without hot running water, without a washer and dryer. She would have liked to have had an oven. And a sewing machine. But to exist on an IVCF salary, and to identify with ordinary Filipinos, she did without.

One day the Magalits received an unexpected gift of several hundred dollars. "An oven at last!" Lety thought. But it was just at that time that Isabelo's brother was knifed—the assassination attempt of a rich neighboring landowner. A severe head injury required immediate surgery, costing 13,000 pesos. Without hesitation or regret, Isabelo and Lety handed over their bonus to their brother, delighted that for once they had the means to help their family in time of need.

In his address at the Urbana Missionary Convention in Illinois in 1979, Magalit said:

> Please do not send us missionaries who insist on a dichotomy between evangelism and social concern. Missionaries who say that evangelism is our main, or even sole concern; ministry to the temporal needs of people we will do also, but only as we have time, later, and as our limited resources allow. Such missionaries make it hard for us to refute the Marxist charge: that Christians promise a pie in the sky for by and by. That Christians who have links with the West are but tools of American imperialism, desiring to perpetuate the pockets of privilege, and

leaving the wretched of the earth to remain wretched! In the long term, unless our love is demonstrated in practical terms of helping meet the need for daily bread, our gospel of love will sound hollow and unconvincing.

Am I asking you to return to the old social gospel? No, for I myself trained as a doctor, but abandoned such a humanitarian profession in order to become a preacher of the gospel to students. But I do ask you to resist—to fight—every dichotomy between preaching the gospel of love and demonstrating that love for needy men and women through our good works. . . . You [Americans] come from the world's richest economy, the largest consumers of the world's goods and its energy. Does the contrast strike you as significant?

. . . The question we all need to face is this: how can we, as followers of Jesus, live more simply today in order that we may be able to give more to meet both temporal and eternal needs of so many millions of people on this planet? I can assure you the question is no less demanding on me than it is on you.[3]

We may be skeptical about economic entanglements with the poor overseas. "It's hopeless. Evangelism is our focus. Aid enriches the rich. We have to tackle America's economic problems first. . . ." But how do these objections stack up against Magalit's plea—which is repeated again and again by intelligent Christian leaders in poorer countries?

What is a reasonable response to the poverty of brothers and sisters around the world? America has a national budget of $221 billion to defend itself from other nations. It has a foreign-aid budget of $4.2 billion to help those nations. Private aid generally is much more successful than government aid: it has much lower operating costs and greater flexibility. On the negative side, it may be paternalistic and may lack rational goal-setting and sustained cumulative thrust. At any rate, we Americans privately give about $2 billion to other countries, including giving to missions.

Money, of course, is not always what poor people need. But the distribution of our treasure is an indication of where our heart is.

The United States has six percent of the world's population, and forty percent of the world's wealth. Much of that wealth comes from other countries, including poor nations: one of our favorite hamburger chains raises its beef on scarce fertile land in Haiti, the poorest nation in the Western hemisphere, where twenty-five percent of the children are severely malnourished.

What is our response to this poverty?

The developing world is shaken by political as well as physical typhoons. There are no easy answers. There are many tough questions. But there are also, perhaps, some positive criteria, and some cities of light, some communities where social and economic transformation is happening.

In this book we will explore these issues, giving special attention to anthropological factors which often have been neglected in other books on Christian development. We don't need to throw our money down a hole. We don't need to support projects so poorly strategized that they backfire and inoculate people against the Gospel. We don't need to strip people of their heritage, leaving them empty and open to seven devils. We don't need to be harmful as serpents and dumb as doves. Every pastor, lay person, and mission committee has a responsibility to be awake, alert, and vigilant, and to ask intelligent, probing questions about the projects they support.

At one level this book contains ideas for implementers, community developers in the field. But at another level this book is for their supporters, who deserve to know what's going on. We who are *not* agriculturalists or nurses, we who stay home, are called to participate in expanding God's kingdom.

It is in Christ, and uniquely in Christ, that God has most fully revealed himself. It is by relationship with God through Christ that people poor and rich find their deepest hungers met, find the surest prescription for health and wholeness, find their special places. Evangelism is essential in today's world. Although there are Christians in every nation, yet there remain many without word of Christ. There are more non-Christians in India and China, for example, than there are Christians in the entire world. There are many "hidden peoples," cut off from any human witness. God is their creator. Their savior. Their lawgiver. Their peacemaker and reconciler. The one who, on their behalf, conquers the powers of darkness, both macrocosmic and microcosmic.

Evangelism, then, is not peripheral, secondary, or outmoded. Certainly mission history (and practice) contains much that is ugly. So does all history. A reading of Christian-Jewish relations appalls us. A reading of the church fathers on women appalls us. Missionaries are in good company: the company of erring Christians who witness erratically to the grace that is greater than we are.

Evangelism remains urgent. This book does not minimize, but rather complements, that vital concern. It explores our response to other areas of God's world where we have had less teaching yet where we must act.

We are called to do this with wisdom as well as love. That means sharing both physical and spiritual resources. Often the needy will respond at both levels, and well-rooted churches will grow along with economic programs.

When John the Baptist found himself in prison at the end of his life, depressed, wondering whether all he had lived for was an illusion, he sent his disciples to Jesus.

They asked, "Are you the Christ, or do we wait for another?"

Jesus answered concretely. "Come and see." And later, "Go tell John what you have seen. The sick are healed, the lame walk, the blind receive their sight."

Today we wonder, "Can Christians substantially help the world's poor?"

In the following chapters the answer is, "Come and see."

---

1. Orlando Costas, "Conversion as a Complex Experience," *Gospel in Context,* July 1978, pp. 14-24.

2. John Sommer, *Beyond Charity: U.S. Voluntary Aid for a Changing Third World* (Washington, D.C.: Overseas Development Council, 1977), p. 44.

3. Isabelo Magalit, "The Messenger's Qualifications," Urbana Missionary Convention, Urbana, Illinois, Dec. 1979.

CHAPTER 1

HEALTH CARE
Helping People Survive

Surely everybody loves a missionary doctor.

Cuddling her child, a Filipino mother on Mindoro Island unwrapped its rags. A pallid, shrunken, listless body emerged. The mother blinked back her tears.

"Can you help?" she begged the missionary.

But the baby was too far gone.

So the mother laid it in a hammock in the house. At first she sat silent and sad. But within half an hour she had begun to laugh hilariously with her friends.

Meanwhile, across the room, her baby was slipping away.

One woman ambled over to the hammock. "Not gone yet," she announced. Some time later, another woman told her two-year-old, "Go and see what's in the hammock. I think you can play with it now."

And they made a football out of the just-dead baby.[1]

This happened not long ago in the mountains of the Philippines. Below these peaks, the jungle steams and the cities bake. But up among the chilly, damp crags, which pierce the sky as far as the eye can see, whole mountainsides ripple with rice terraces, many of them taller than a man. They have been called the eighth wonder of the world. In this land of mudslides, strong, big-chested villagers maintain the terraces. A complex irrigation system bathes the delicate rice seedlings, distributing water fairly, as it has for centuries.

But this is no Eden. Hepatitis, typhus, malaria, cholera, and gastroenteritis attack these people. Too many children and adults operate at half their capacity. Too many babies die. To bear it, when there is no alternative, these people may develop a hard shell. Like the mother who joked while her baby died.

Yet parents can't forget the clinging little fingers, the trusting smiles, the fresh skin and wide-awake eyes that both exhausted

11

them and made them young again. So they try herbal medicines.
And they pray to God in the only ways they know how. For example, like the people of Old Testament times, they offer blood
sacrifices.

Great horns curving, a ponderous, humpbacked water buffalo
is led out. Every man around pulls out a knife. One slash, and a
bloody red wound oozes on the buffalo's buttock. Someone has
sliced off part of his haunch. He bellows, pivots, and charges, but a
dozen men stab him from behind. One man even bayonets another
by accident. While the buffalo cries and tries to defend himself,
blood spurts out of gaping holes in his body, and more hunks of his
flesh are chopped off. Finally he sinks to his knees. The gods have a
sacrifice. Will they care enough to heal the sickness that prompted
this gore?

Sacrifices are expensive. They keep people in debt. A water
buffalo is a Filipino farmer's tractor, without any bills for high-
octane fuel. Yet a Bontoc Filipino may offer up fifteen water buffa-
loes in one sacrifice. Then he scrimps and struggles for years to
repay his creditors. He is like the people described by the writer of
Hebrews who were "all their lifetime subject to bondage, through
fear of death" (Heb. 2:15), and through fear of the spirits and gods
that hold life and death in their hands.

What is the kingdom of God to the mountain people of the
Philippines? Healing their sicknesses is part of it. So on the big,
rugged frontier island of Mindanao, René Sison coordinates a
branch of Medical Ambassadors. Sison committed himself to Jesus
Christ in medical school. When he changed schools a few years
later, he met a woman classmate who was also a Christian. They
married, and together they determined to go where there were
few doctors. In the barely accessible mountains of Mindanao, she
set up a clinic. From that base Sison travels to remote tribal areas.
Today he coordinates at least five Christian satellite clinics, bringing kingdom healing to the backwoods so that people don't have
to be so apparently callous about their babies dying. This is the
front line for the Medical Ambassadors, an indigenous, Manila-
based organization.

Light years away is metropolitan Manila. Here air conditioners
hum. Tourist hotels scrape the sky and jostle for a view of the bay.
Capital flows in, drawn by stability enforced by martial law and
favorable terms for foreign investors. Canny local businessmen

play the money market. Near the university, public administration buildings, bright white, are framed in space and greenery along palm-lined avenues. In the Manila Hotel, where French and Spanish conversations drift through the halls and around the swimming pool, fine specimens of exotica from the rugged mountain people drape the walls. The best bands and singers in Asia make music throb in the supper clubs. This is Manila, pearl of the Orient, center of the spice trade between China and Mexico through the famous Acapulco galleon run, an undeniably romantic blend of Malay, Chinese, European, and American cultures.

Yet not far across the city's canals, between Manila Bay, famous for its spectacular sunsets, and the skyscrapers of high finance, is Barrio Mandaragat. Here eight to ten thousand Filipinos squeeze into nine acres between the billowing, sewage-filled waves and a mountain of putrid garbage covering fifty acres. Every day ninety garbage trucks vomit forth new loads. During high tide, the barrio floods. There are no streets, only muddy, unlit alleys. Gastroenteritis gradually infects whole families.

Many of the *Manilenos* in this barrio have come from the island of Samar; they finally had had all the typhoons they could take. More recently, the New People's Army, an illegal Marxist group, had invaded their hinterland. Manila spelled hope—they thought.

But they couldn't find jobs.

Now husbands and fathers block the paths in the afternoon. They are drunk, or drinking. Tattoos cover many arms and shoulders—signs of time spent in jail.

How do families make ends meet? Crawling over the mountain, sifting through the stinking garbage for something saleable, supports them. But not very well. In this urban community where everything must be bought, the total average family income is about forty-five dollars a month.

What is the kingdom of God to the people of Barrio Mandaragat? Part of it is a clinic and nutrition program for over two hundred malnourished preschoolers.

One good meal daily. Stories, singing, games. Periodic deworming. Immunizations. Chest x-rays. Regular clinic hours. Even Bible studies for the mothers of these preschoolers. All are part of the program.

Members of Balut Christian Church—just across the highway physically, but miles away socially—have gotten up enough courage to walk into the lawless barrio and escort families to church. For some mothers, Jesus Christ has meant a change in the way they live. They've quit criticizing and cursing. Some fathers have stopped drinking. One of the first children to "graduate" from this program and enroll in school has been nominated as the model student in his class in a school outside the slum.

In spite of local poverty, those who run the program are working to gain local support for fifty percent of the budget. "Can you give a contribution?" every patient is asked. Drugs don't cost much, but the minimal charge for them helps. Most of the children are sponsored individually through a group called Advancing the Ministry of the Gospel.

This clinic follows the healing example of Jesus. In many other countries, too, Christians have pioneered in medicine. John Wesley founded the first free medical dispensary in England. In China, as early as 1914, there were more than a million patients in missionary hospitals. Christians there built schools for the deaf, devised a Braille system for Mandarin-speaking people, and administered efforts to relieve famine. Ninety-two foreign Christian women with M.D.'s were assigned posts throughout China in 1914. In India, the secular *Illustrated Weekly* reports, "Christian endeavour has given India . . . 620 hospitals, 670 dispensaries, 86 leprosy centers. . . . What other community has done as much for our country?"[2]

Leprosy scares people. Just a few years ago, a teenage girl in the Midwest discovered she had leprosy. Her books, school desk, and chair were burned. Townspeople wanted her out. So the sheriff, pistol hanging from his hip, escorted her like a criminal to the government leprosy hospital in Louisiana.[3]

Fear made these people behave less kindly than they might have. When he was on earth, Jesus touched lepers, and Christians try to reach out as he did. Today most of the medical and rehabilitative work among lepers throughout the world is in Christian hands.

Countries like Afghanistan and Nepal, closed to foreign missions, get much of their top medical care from foreign Christians. To support such programs, Americans give more than one billion dollars a year in private assistance to the Third World.

Surely everybody loves a missionary doctor. Or do they?

In fact, some don't. Some anthropologists, for example, argue that modern medicine often leaves people worse off than they were before. F. Landa Jocano, chairman of the Department of Anthropology at the University of the Philippines, explains,

> Bringing medicine to the mountain peoples for a day or so, or even a week, and then leaving them to fend for themselves for the rest of the year is not only administratively wrong but morally challenging. I have seen, on the basis of my ten years' research experience in various sections of the country, how short-term welfare programs alienate people from their cultural know-how and social relations with the local healers, so that, when the benefactors leave, readjustments to the normal run of life become difficult. First, they begin to doubt the skill of their healers and the effectiveness of their folk medicine. Second, modern medicine is not readily available. The nearest drug store—as among the Sulod of Central Panay—is more than a week's walk. Third, if modern medicines are available—like pain pills—these are used indiscriminately for all known illnesses and when a particular disease is not cured doubts as to the effectiveness of modern medicine follow and anxiety becomes dominant in the minds of those concerned. And fourth, often the change agent, in spite of his sincerity to help, is viewed by the local healer as a competitor. Thus those who come to him for assistance lose the friendship of the herb doctor who often refuses to attend to such patients when the change agent is gone.[4]

Beyond the anthropologists, nationalists charge that missionary medics are out to create bigger markets for Western drug companies. Preposterous? Whatever the missionaries' unwitting role, U.S. drug companies do compete in a cutthroat way overseas. In *Cry of the People,* a book about the Roman Catholic Church in Latin America, Penny Lernoux documents this. Through "transfer pricing"—in which a company artificially manipulates the costs of supplies that it sells to its own subsidiaries in various nations—American drugs in Latin America cost twenty to thirty percent more than the same drugs cost when they come from another country. Monopoly contracts or patents held by U.S. drug companies keep competition out. They also suppress local drug production. Since a developing country may spend fifty to sixty percent of its health budget on drugs (compared with fifteen to twenty percent in an industrialized country), this monopolist overpricing is disastrous.

Worse still is the "dumping" of drugs known to be dangerous—
like thalidomide—overseas. According to Lernoux,

> Altogether, four hundred drugs on sale in Brazil have been
> condemned as dangerous by the Medical Association of Rio de
> Janeiro, and a good many of them are sold by the foreign com-
> panies that control 80 per cent of the country's pharmaceutical
> business. . . . Among them is an antique drug called cincho-
> phen, introduced in 1902 as a treatment for gout, but long
> since abandoned in the United States and Europe because it can
> cause fatal hepatitis. It is still marketed by Abbott under the
> brand name Cincofeno to "stimulate the elimination of uric
> acid." A similarly dangerous drug, chloramphenicol, known for
> more than twenty years to cause the fatal blood disease aplastic
> anemia, is marketed by Dow Chemical, USV-Grossman, and
> Parke-Davis. According to studies by a group of Colombian
> doctors in Bogota and Cali, the introduction of chlorampheni-
> col led to "aplastic anemia becoming a dreadfully common
> disease" in Colombia. Although Parke-Davis has paid over $1
> million in damages in the United States for failing to warn users
> that the antibiotic Chloromycetin can produce undesirable side
> effects, it continues to promote this drug in several developing
> countries with no warning whatsoever of the six circumstances
> under which the drug should not be used. . . .
> One of the most popular drugs sold in Latin America is
> dipyrone. . . . Both the U.S. Government and the American
> Medical Association restrict its use "as the last resort to reduce
> fever when safer measures have failed" because it can cause
> fatal blood diseases. . . . Yet this drug is sold everywhere in Latin
> America as a harmless pain-killer and its advertising leads the
> customer to believe that it is safe for small children. In Colom-
> bia, where it is called Conmel, it ranks twentieth on a list of
> best-selling drugs.[5]

Nationalists object to missionary medics who, however innocently,
enlarge the market for such drug rackets.

Like anthropologists and nationalists, economists also raise eye-
brows at missionary medicine.

Several years ago, tuberculosis was the major scourge in one
group of Pacific islands. One day, however, the chief medical
officer there got an inspiration. He went to the governor's office
and strode in confidently.

"Sir," he said, "I believe I've thought of a way to eradicate TB from these islands."

"Oh? What's that?" the governor asked.

"Well—if I may use this map here—you see these three un-inhabited islands? Let's call them A, B, and C. Now suppose we were to round up all the cases of TB in the population. We'd isolate the most severe cases on island A, the medium ones on island B, and the light ones on island C. Gradually, as they got well, we'd feed them back into the population. And our problems would be over. Given time, I believe the disease would be very nearly wiped out."

The governor was quiet for a minute, then spoke. "A great plan," he said. "But we're certainly not going to implement it."

"Why not?" the startled doctor demanded.

"Because if we didn't have TB in these islands, the land base couldn't possibly support the population," explained the governor.

In fact, although the government did not launch any serious campaign against TB, in a few years the population had so out-stripped the resource base that large numbers of people had to be relocated on other islands thousands of miles away.

Economists point out that modern medicine keeps more people alive than poor countries can support. In the West, industry devel-oped before modern medicine, so Western economies could sup-port increased populations. But to poor countries today we send doctors before we send businessmen. Medicine precedes eco-nomic growth.

Are these doctors saving millions for a malnourished half-life? Are they making more misery rather than alleviating it?

These are the objections of intellectuals. But ordinary people too are suspicious of missionary doctors when they feel that medi-cine is scratching where they don't itch, answering questions that they are not asking and leaving unanswered questions that plague them.

In one Middle Eastern village described by Afif Tannous of the Department of State, people were continually being laid low by typhoid, malaria, and dysentery. The babies died almost as fast as the mosquitoes.

The culprit? A tiny spring that meandered into a stagnant pool. Here mothers scooped up family drinking water. Here they also scrubbed clothes. And here children bathed—alongside cows, goats, sheep, and donkeys.

The solution? Covering the well and installing a pump. When a medical team proposed this, the villagers seemed agreeable. But on the day chosen for digging at the site, no one showed up. Eventually the truth came out: the people didn't want a pump.

Why? Prodded, the villagers explained:

"Our fathers, grandfathers, and great grandfathers drank from this water as it is, and I don't see why we should make a change now."

"You say that you want to install a pump at the spring; but I for one have never seen a pump, nor do I know what might happen if it should be put there."

"I tell you what will happen. The water will flow out so fast that the spring will dry up in no time."

"Not only that, but the iron pipe will spoil the taste of the water for us and for our animals."

"You So and So," put in one of Jibrail's elders, who are much more advanced than the people of [the village in question], "do you like the taste of dung in your water better?"

"Well, I admit it is bad; but we and our animals are at least used to it."

"You have told us that the water is the cause of our illness and of our children's death. I do not believe that, and I can't see how it could be. To tell you the truth, I believe that the matter of life and death is in Allah's hands, and we cannot do much about it."

"One more thing. We don't understand why you should go to all this trouble. Why are you so concerned about us?"

"You say that the pump will save our women much effort and time. If that happens, what are they going to do with themselves all day long?"[6]

Not everybody welcomes modern medicine. Even common people sometimes are skeptical. Some of their objections are economic. Others have to do with social relations. Still others are related to their world view.

Take economic objections, for example. Juan Flavier is now director of the International Institute of Rural Reconstruction. He describes how, early in his career, as a young doctor in the Philippine Rural Reconstruction Movement, he was awakened one night.

"Pssst!"

"Who's there?"

"It's me, sir. I'm sorry to disturb you, but my baby is sick. Will you come?"

After traveling several kilometers to a bamboo hut, Flavier examined the child and diagnosed pneumonia.

"Penicillin," he said. "Could someone go to the drugstore?"

A silence fell.

"Doctor, at this time of night the drugstore in town won't open for anybody, for fear of thieves," the father said.

Suddenly the child suffered a convulsion.

"We need some ice," Flavier said automatically.

Another silence.

"Sir, ice is only available in this village once a year. At fiesta time."

Flavier's training had not prepared him for this. He was mentally wringing his hands when a wizened grandmother tottered up and placed a small bundle on the child's forehead. "This is what we use here," she said.

The fever dropped.

The bundle turned out to be pieces of chopped leaf sheaths from the trunk of a banana tree, which are extremely porous. When soaked in water, they have a cooling effect.[7]

Economic factors are basic. As an old Filipino farmer explained during a toilet-building campaign aimed at wiping out worms, "Dr. Flavier, toilets are fine. But in this barrio, our problem is not what comes out below. Our problem is lack of what goes into our mouths."

How much water is available for sanitation? How far do the people live from clinics? How convenient is transportation? How many medics are available? These are economic questions. When trained personnel are scarce, local middle-aged women may be taught to diagnose ailments by symptom and to supervise the dispensing of simple medications, selling the drugs at cost in order to keep the medicine chest stocked. Dr. Carroll Berhorst's Guatemalan clinic has trained over seventy such paramedics. Their continuing education includes three-day courses every month, with a written exam. If they fail, they face the shame of not being able to get any medications to take home to their village for the rest of the month. Each village chooses its own paramedic, and because the people feel they have an investment in her, they push her to study and keep up her standards.

Professional pride may balk at the primitive care poor people can afford to support. We can learn from Dr. Tom Dooley, who ran a simple clinic in Laos before he died of leukemia.

"People accuse me of practicing nineteenth-century medicine," he said. "They are correct. I did practice nineteenth-century medicine, and this was just fine. Upon my departure, our indigenous personnel would practice eighteenth-century medicine. Good, this is progress, since most of the villagers live in the fifteenth century."[8]

But economic issues are not the only issues. People in poor countries also wonder, "Does modern medicine take human relationships seriously?"

When we Americans first go to a doctor, he asks questions about our past health; he calls it taking a "physical history." Traditional native healers, however, seek not only a physical history but also a social history. Who has quarreled with the patient? Whom does he have a grudge against? Whom is he jealous of? What are the natural lines of tension in this society? The native healer takes all these factors into account in his diagnosis. He faces them head-on if they apply to the case. In so doing, he sometimes defuses an explosive situation.

A Christian businessman in Africa had supported his church generously for years. But treasurer after treasurer had absconded with the funds. Finally he complained to a missionary. The missionary checked with a Christian anthropologist. "How can we nurture more faithful church treasurers?" he asked.

"That's not the first question," the anthropologist answered. "You need to get that businessman out here for counseling right now."

"Why?"

"Well, if he wasn't a Christian, that businessman would be performing sorcery against the last treasurer," the anthropologist explained. "Eventually a native healer would find it out, get the buried resentments out into the open, and get the thief to make reparation. But, since he's a Christian, this businessman probably doesn't know how to deal with his murderous feelings. You mentioned that he had a stomach pain? That's serious. He's turning his aggression in on himself."

"So what do we do?"

"He needs counsel. Immediately. Otherwise it's going to eat away inside him. Better get him out here right away."

But the missionary wanted to check out some details first. Several days later he went to the businessman's house.

In tears, the African's wife met him at the door. "You are too late," she sobbed. "My husband's stomach pain got worse and worse. Yesterday he died."[9]

Does our medicine take personal relationships this seriously? One study of medical patients in England suggests that forty percent have symptoms with a psychological basis. Other studies hint at higher percentages. Our ulcers, migraines, skin eruptions, weight problems, and heart palpitations often speak volumes about our relationships. The apostle Paul wrote that he bore in his body the marks of the Lord Jesus. Do we? Or do we often bear instead very different marks—marks of lovelessness toward ourselves, toward God, toward others? The apostle John wrote that the person who doesn't love his brother abides in death. Does this have any medical significance for us? Is it possible that we kill ourselves off before our time because of our resentments and angers? Or is this too embarrassing to consider—because it has too many implications for our own self-centered neuroses? At any rate, many common people around the world ask that relationships be taken seriously. That guilt be taken seriously. That we acknowledge that social interaction can have physical effects.

In addition, people in developing countries generally want healing to occur within the context of community support. Do we take this into account? Do we allow patients' relatives to sleep alongside them in the hospital and to cook their hospital food? Do we ask the people of a community to choose their own trainee for the paramedic program, so that they will have an investment in the program, a sense of responsibility for the trainee? Do we care enough to find out what the local social structures are?

Consider the findings of one recent missionary report:

There is absolutely no community spirit here. The houses are scattered all over. Very few of the children attend school. There is no sanitary water supply and there are no toilets. There is no one to give health care and the people just don't seem to want to try to follow directions. We try to teach just simple things like hygiene and treatment using local measures such as washing wounds with salt water and taking oral fluids when a baby has a fever but often we are unsuccessful because of their tribal beliefs. They drink very little water because of the old belief that it would slow down a warrior chasing his enemy. Their lives are often ruled by spirits and there are many things that are taboo. Sometimes if someone dies or is sick during a harvest time they will completely abandon the crop because they think they may have offended the spirits. But [we] have been patient and have started construction on the "bridge." The love of Christ and modern medicine have teamed up to span the river but much more time and effort will be needed.

This was written about the broad-shouldered, self-assured Ifugao people, who have molded the Philippine rice terraces, managing a breathtakingly complex irrigation system for centuries without the need for any central government. Yet where in this missionary report is there an appreciation of Ifugao community structures?

Caring about these structures also means finding out who the local health specialists are and consulting them. Bruce Olson, who has lived for almost twenty years with the Motilones of the South American jungle, illustrates how important this is.

After Bruce got to know the Motilones, he tried to introduce some simple medicines into their stock of remedies. But the people wouldn't touch them. "You white men have your own medicines," they said, "and we have ours."

One day an epidemic of pinkeye swept through the long house. Soon everybody had burning, running eyes. Bruce was ready to explode with frustration. In his medical kit was a simple antibiotic that would tackle the disease, but the people wouldn't use it.

Finally, desperate, Bruce touched a finger to a Motilone friend's eye, then to his own. In five days, he too had a raging case of pinkeye. Then he went to the native healer.

"Auntie, can you please give me something for my eyes? They're burning," he pleaded.

"Bruce, I wish I could help you," she answered. "But I've tried every herb and chant I know. Nothing works. I'm worn out."

Bruce pulled a tube of ointment out of his back pocket. "Well, Auntie, I do have some white man's medicine. I wonder if you would be willing to smear some on my eyes?" She complied.

Bruce's pinkeye cleared up in a few days, and he rushed back to the healer. "Auntie, look! You've cured my eyes!"

She was impressed.

"Why don't you try this potion on some of the others?" Bruce added.

"Nothing lost," thought the healer. She tried it, and it worked. In three days she had cured everybody. As a result, she began to listen to Bruce's health suggestions. She was willing to look through his primitive microscope, and she marveled at the wiggling demons that she had always known were responsible for disease. When the people periodically beat a long house to exorcise spirits, she was willing now to use disinfectants as well. Within a few years the Motilones were running eight clinics. They were doing both the diagnoses and the treatments; they were giving the injections. Spanish-speaking settlers were streaming to their clinics by the thousands.[10]

Besides wanting medical treatment that is economically realistic and socially responsible, people also want something that makes sense. This means explaining treatment in their terms. People aren't empty cups, waiting to be filled with our knowledge. They already have ideas about causes of and treatments for certain sicknesses. To make them believe in our medicine, we must relate it to their indigenous world view and values, including their myths, their rituals, their taboos, and their ideas of modesty.

Many Latin Americans have grown up convinced that certain foods and medicines, regardless of their temperature, are "hot." Others are "cold." In Peru, for example, eggs, bread, hen meat, and apples are "hot." Cheese, potatoes, turkey, and onions are "cold." Similarly, aspirin, vitamins, and Kaopectate are "hot." But Alka-Seltzer, sulfa, penicillin, and milk of magnesia are "cold."

When these people get sick, they want their food and medicine to offset their physical condition. For example, pregnant women, who are in a "hot" state, are supposed to avoid "hot" foods.

Imagine, then, the shock of a patient with a "hot" disease who receives a prescription for "hot" penicillin. Or who is served "hot" foods on a hospital diet. Why should he cooperate with such irrational treatment? If he were given more "sensible" medication and food, the patient would follow his regimen much more willingly and confidently.

Consider a positive example. A health program in Zaire began with what the people knew. To them, disease represented social disruption. Somebody was angry, either a neighbor or a spirit. Whether the angry person knew it or not, his feeling exploded in sorcery, which made others sick. Disease always began with the wrath of one person, and spread invisibly.

How could one build on these beliefs? The medical team said, "Yes, disease passes from person to person. Yes, you can transmit it unwittingly. But you can also transmit it willfully. If you know that you should be vaccinated but you chicken out, if you know you should use a toilet but you use a field, then you purposely expose your neighbors to danger."

"Yes, God created the world. But he is not distant, as you have been taught. Instead, he is very curious about what we do. In fact, he holds us responsible for the condition of our neighborhood. God is concerned for the health of his people."

Village church-leaders took charge of these health programs. Within four years, eighty villages in Zaire adopted radically different health habits. The churches also grew greatly in number, influence, and respect.[11]

Patients want therapy that makes sense. Let us respect this. Whatever a people's world view, they are made in the image of God. They are capable of living full, significant lives. No one would question John Wesley's intelligence or impact. Yet in 1780 he wrote in his journal,

> *Thur. 14.* I read prayers and preached in Clutton church; but it was with great difficulty, because of my hoarseness, which so increased, that in four and twenty hours I could scarce speak at all. At night I used my never-failing remedy, bruised garlick applied to the soles of the feet. This cured my hoarseness in six hours; and in one hour it cured my lumbago, the pain in the small of my back, which I had had ever since I came from Cornwall.[12]

Apparently modern medicine isn't everything. In fact, folk therapy answers broader questions in many societies than scientific medicine does in ours. We might even say that folk medicine often provides a theology of suffering. Our germ-oriented medicine answers the question "How?" But many people are asking, "Why?" As one well-educated African put it, "'It may be quite true that typhus is carried by lice. But who sent the infected louse? Why did it bite one man and not another?'"[13]

We ask this kind of question, too. Anyone in Western society who is afflicted with cancer asks, "Why? Why me? Why now?" But we've learned not to turn to doctors for answers to these questions. We turn to psychologists, to our church, to philosophy, to Dear Abby, to sensitivity groups.

Non-Westerners, however, haven't learned to divide up therapy like this. They believe that in order to marshal their physical resources, they need some idea of what's going on. If they can't make any sense of this adverse thing that's happened to them, they're likely to sink into hopelessness, into fatalism.

Native healers in these cultures come to the rescue. Sometimes through myth, sometimes through ritual, sometimes through folk psychology, they help patients understand why they are suffering. Then they set up a regimen to mobilize and channel the patients' restless energies in a therapeutic direction.

Why *do* people suffer? What can we Christians say? Suffering refines us. It educates us. It builds character. It helps us grow. It reveals new levels of God's personal power and love. In our Christian heritage, we can learn something from Daniel, held in captivity. Habakkuk, surveying the ruin of Israel. Paul, enduring his thorn in the flesh. Our Lord Jesus, whose face indicated to people that he was despised, rejected, acquainted with grief, stricken, smitten of God, and afflicted. Can we share these models in everyday language with our patients, and so offer a theology of suffering—an answer to "Why?"—starting from a Christian view of man?

In medicine, as in every other area of development, people demand not only methods but also meaning and motivation. The Agency for International Development, a secular agency of the U.S. government, cannot provide this. A Christian effort can. Beyond meaning, sick people also demand power—including supernatural power. They are ready to tap into all the supernatural power they can find. Pentecostal churches are mushrooming around the world; a big part of their attraction is healing. We must face the fact that when people are in trouble, they long to grab hold of all available power. In such situations, non-Westerners find our scientific naturalism deflating.

An example is provided by the well-loved missionary serving a Latin American tribe. One morning he discovered that the Christians among the people had held a prayer meeting for a sick member the night before.

"You should have told me," the missionary remarked to one of
the men. "I would have liked to come."

After a moment's hesitation, his friend answered gently, "Well,
we don't know whether you really believe that God can heal."

The missionary was cut to the quick. Faced with sickness or
injury, he realized, he tended to offer physical and pharmaceutical
help. His friends didn't see him as a man immersed in prayer. To
them this implied that his presence at their prayer meeting might
squelch its effectiveness.

The challenge to us is this: Are the personnel in a typical mission hospital people of faith? People of prayer? People so aware of
and filled with the presence of God that their lives transmit a
certain supernatural peace and power and authority to their patients? So that the Creator of the universe comes with them into
the sickroom?

A Muslim prays five times a day, wherever he is. A pagan prays
before he plants a field, before he harvests, before he builds a
house. When we go to other countries, we must stop our Western
compartmentalizing of the secular and the sacred. Increasingly
our office personnel need to learn to stop and pray with colleagues right in the middle of managerial problems. Our agriculturalists need to stand on dikes between fields and pray for
protection for the crops. We need to come out of our Western
closets and live at a new level of expectancy.

To be economically realistic, socially responsible, and prescrip-
tively sensible to cultures beyond ours—these are large demands
to make of a medical program. Often we don't meet them. Yet
with all its shortcomings, medical care still is an expression of
Christ's love.

It may be true that not everyone loves a missionary doctor. It
may be true that the participants in mission health programs need
to take a long look at themselves and change their strategies.

It may be true that the workers in the program in Barrio Mandaragat should train and place fathers in jobs to give the children
in the clinic more stable homes and role models. Possibly they
should discontinue Bible studies for the nearly illiterate mothers,
and instead put on biblical dramas every Saturday night in the
barrio, performed by the youth of the Balut Christian Church.
Undoubtedly the program personnel ought to listen more to what

the people themselves think their problems are, and what might be solutions and alternatives.

Yet take the health program in Barrio Mandaragat[14] just as it is. Sixty of the most malnourished children in the barrio drifted listlessly through the door of the clinic the first day. They were so docile, so good, the staff remembers. Today 150 youngsters are healthy enough to compare with the bouncing, noisy rascals you find in any preschool. They have a chance that the mother on Mindoro Island will never see her baby have.

If one of these was your child, wouldn't this be a sign of the kingdom to you?

---

1. Caroline Stickley, *Broken Snare* (Sevenoaks, Kent: Overseas Missionary Fellowship, 1975), pp. 129-130.

2. *Illustrated Weekly,* Dec. 28, 1969.

3. Gene Phillips, "One Hundred Years of Ministry to Lepers," *Christianity Today,* Sept. 1973, p. 48.

4. F. Landa Jocano, "Humanitarianism and Applied Change: The Case of Filipino Ethnic Minorities," *Solidarity,* May 1969.

5. Penny Lernoux, *Cry of the People* (Garden City, N.Y.: Doubleday, 1980), pp. 218-219.

6. Afif Tannous, *Extension Work among the Arab Fellahin* (Foreign Service Institute, Department of State, 1951), quoted in Earl Bell, *Social Foundations of Human Behavior* (New York: Harper and Row, 1961), pp. 492-493.

7. Juan Flavier, *Doctor to the Barrios* (Quezon City, the Philippines: New Day Publishers, 1970), pp. 142-145.

8. Thomas Dooley, *The Edge of Tomorrow* (New York: Farrar, Straus, and Cudahy, 1958), p. 54.

9. Jacob Loewen, "Mission Churches, Independent Churches, and Felt Needs in Africa," *Missiology,* Oct. 1976, pp. 407-408.

10. Bruce Olson, *For This Cross I'll Kill You* (Carol Stream, Ill.: Creation House, 1973), pp. 146-150.

11. Daniel Fountain, "The Church and Cross-Cultural Communication in Public Health: A Project in Zaire," *Missiology,* Jan. 1975, pp. 103-112.

12. John Wesley, *The Journal of John Wesley,* ed. Nehemiah Curnock (London: Epworth Press, 1938), VI, 294.

13. Monica Wilson, "Witch Beliefs and Social Structure," *American Journal of Sociology,* 1951, pp. 307-313.

14. As this book goes to press, the Philippine government has razed the garbage mound and relocated the squatters in an area distant from urban resources. However, the child nutrition ministry has followed the squatters.

CHAPTER 2

AGRICULTURE
Helping People Feed Themselves

"**W**HY won't the farmers around here buy my product?" an insecticide salesman once complained to Juan Flavier, who was then director of the Philippine Rural Reconstruction Institute. "Can't the farmers even see their fields full of white heads? Don't they realize they're infested with stem-borer disease?"

"Stem-borer? What's that?" Flavier asked.

"An insect that bores into the stalk of a rice plant. No nutrients reach the kernel. It develops empty—just a white husk. Look around. You can see the white heads in almost any field near here."

Flavier invited the salesman to accompany him on one of his regular visits to the fields that afternoon. Before long, they were walking on a dike between fields. Nearby, two farmers were weeding.

Flavier stopped. "Sir," he called out to the nearest farmer, "could you tell me why those rice husks are white?"

The farmer straightened up. "Those are due to thunder during planting season," he answered. "It frightens the rice."

Flavier thanked him, and went on. The salesman shook his head.

A little later they took time to chat with an old woman. She was winnowing newly harvested rice, tossing it up into the air from a flat basket again and again.

"Why are those rice husks white?" Flavier asked her.

"Oh, you know my nephew, Berto," she cackled. "It's all his fault. He's toothless. I warn him and warn him not to laugh when he sows the rice. But it's no use. He can't help it. So the rice comes up toothless."

As the two men walked away, the salesman exploded, "Well, I can see why they won't buy my insecticide, if they don't even believe in the stem-borer!"

"There are a few more factors you need to consider," Flavier added. "You aren't the first insecticide salesman here. A few years ago, a farmer washed his sprayer in the river. The fish died. The frogs died. The ducks died. Even a water buffalo died downstream. In another case, when a farmer sprayed his fields, all the insects went to his neighbor's fields. Neither of these innovative farmers won a popularity contest, you can be sure."[1]

What can we do to feed the hungry? We can help poor countries improve their agriculture. It's not easy, as the experience of the insecticide salesman shows. But it is an obvious step. While farmers in many parts of the world shake their heads over their withered vegetable patches, the average American farmer now raises enough crops to feed seventy-five people. (The average Soviet farmer raises enough to feed ten.) Almost half of the world's corn, two-thirds of its soybeans, and more than a tenth of its wheat are grown in the United States. Of America's 413 million acres of crop land, about one-fourth now are planted with crops meant for sale overseas. America exports more wheat, corn, sorghum, barley, and oats than all other countries combined.[2]

Certainly America could help a lot of hungry people by sending them food. The catch is that those hungry people would just need more food next year. And the next. And the next.

In the long run, hungry people need more than charity; they need the skills and the land and the capital to produce their own food and goods.

Some poor farmers need a dependable water supply. Others may need training, farm implements, seeds, new hybrid breeds, animal stock, marketing networks, roads, or agronomists' advice. Could we not share some of our sophisticated agricultural know-how with them? Could we not help them become self-supporting?

In 1943, scientists in Mexico began to try to breed high-yielding varieties of corn, wheat, and beans. Eventually they succeeded. Other breakthroughs followed, like the "miracle rice" developed in the Philippines. These advancements triggered what was called the Green Revolution. By 1971, using these varieties of grain, several countries, including India and the Philippines, were producing self-sustaining quantities of wheat and rice. Norman Borlaug won the Nobel Peace Prize in 1970 for pioneering this revolution. Though weather, fuel, and fertilizer crises in the later 1970's hurt production, the gains have been undeniably impressive.

When God has made us managers of comparatively vast resources, does he delight in our dribbling out haphazard doses of charity? Or does he want instead modern Josephs who will prevent death by famine by tackling society's economic problems on a large scale? And Daniels who will reorganize nations?

Cambodia is a case in point. Genocide marked the Pol Pot regime, which began in 1975. Several million Cambodians were killed. Hundreds of thousands fled to refugee camps in Thailand. Once the Pol Pot regime was overthrown, however, many Cambodians were willing to try to rebuild their lives in their own land. But they had lost their farming equipment and, more significantly, their seed supplies. They faced starvation if they went back.

In the spring of 1980, several Christian agencies decided to "capitalize" Cambodian farmers with rice seed. At the Thai border they gave a 66-pound bag of seed rice, along with a 44-pound bag of table rice, to every Cambodian farmer over age twelve who showed up. Some Cambodians traveled as far as 120 miles to collect the supplies.

These Christian organizations also gave out food at the official government receiving-point, the harbor of Phnom Penh. But bottlenecks there meant waste. What a relief it was to get special permission for this "Project Landbridge," and to give bags of seeds directly to those who would use them. Reports that have filtered back from inside Cambodia indicate that very little of this rice has been stolen by unscrupulous officials.

Giving Cambodian farmers seed meant they would be able to help themselves in the future. Toward the same end, some Christian groups have provided refugee camps in Thailand with seeds, chickens, and pigs so that the refugees can raise their own food. Recently, when Thailand was deluged by its worst floods in a hundred years, gardens planted with donated seeds supplied whole camps with food. "You'll never know how many lives were saved by the vegetable gardens," one camp official told a visiting American.

In addition, many Thai outside the camps, inspired by the gardens they saw beyond the camp fences, planted their own gardens. So many vegetables were grown that the markets overflowed with produce. Prices dropped, and the poorest of the poor were able to buy vital foods. All because Christians cared enough to send a few basic agricultural supplies.

In Bangladesh, a Christian organization named HEED has discovered that nearly .8 million people in one region suffer from
night blindness. This has been traced to a deficiency of vitamin A
in their diet. More than eighty percent of the people also suffer
from deficiencies of riboflavin, vitamin C, and iron. But agriculturalists working with HEED have discovered that local plants like
laksak, palongsak, mulasak, and *laisak* are rich in these very
nutrients. HEED's simple vegetable gardens are going to do won-
ders for the health of the people.

In Colombia, an indigenous Christian organization named
Accion Unida has bettered the economic lives of thousands of
families. It began with the Landero family. A tavern-owner and
brothel-keeper, Victor Landero lived alternately with three mis-
tresses. He came to know Christ through a traveling Colombian
evangelist and a Bible. He was an enthusiastic—and unusual—
convert. To everyone he met he told his good news—at first, with a
bottle in one hand and a Bible in the other. Hundreds of families
turned to Christ before any missionaries piloted dugout canoes to
this isolated part of the jungle. Few of the people could read, but
many had excellent memories and could quote long passages of
the Bible.

Some time later, the missionary David Howard asked Victor
about his "church-planting plan":

> Until then, I hadn't thought much about having such a "plan"
> [Victor remembers]. But as we talked, it began to come into
> focus.
>
> I told him, "When I first go into a village, I trust God to
> provide open hearts for His message. He always does that, and
> several people receive Jesus.
>
> "I return to that place on a regular basis. And, each time,
> more people come to Christ. I remain in each place for quite a
> while to teach them from the Scriptures: how to live as believ-
> ers and how to depend upon Jesus. I teach them these things
> very thoroughly."
>
> [Howard] asked, "How many times do you visit a group like
> this before a church becomes established?"
>
> "Five times, usually."
>
> "Only five times?" he asked.
>
> "Yes. Five visits are usually enough."
>
> He was amazed. To me it seemed perfectly natural for us
> simply to serve as spokesmen for the Holy Spirit and to let Him
> take over. It never occurred to us that He would not do so.[3]

But Victor's brother, Gregorio, was troubled. A traveling evangelist, he stayed in people's homes. At one home one day, the woman of the house set the table at mealtime with just one plate.

"How about the others in the family?" Gregorio asked. "Have they eaten?"

"Don't worry about them," she said. "You eat."

She served him one egg and some yucca starch. He bowed his head. When he looked up, four little children were gathered around the table. Four pairs of eyes were fixed on his egg.

Gregorio couldn't eat.

He divided the egg four ways. The children wolfed it down as though they hadn't eaten for days. Gregorio left that place determined to do something about hunger.

With the help of the Latin American Mission, he incorporated *Accion Unida*. He started teaching his people that God has made us stewards of this earth. Then, on soil worn out from slash-and-burn cultivation, he got Christian agronomists to teach the farmers how to rotate crops. They learned to grow more profitable plants, like pineapples and coconuts. A poultry-raising project followed. Then came home industries that produced furniture, tapestries, hammocks, and sandals. Gregorio's *Accion Unida* trains the craftsmen, demonstrates how to build necessary equipment, finds sources of raw materials, and develops markets. Since 1981, *Accion Unida* has been pioneering in water resource development, and has invested in a motor pump. Now, if a local community will install an irrigation system that will pay for the transportation of the pump, *Accion Unida* will loan them the machine. Since this economic uplift began, many families have turned to Jesus.

If agriculturalists can bring good news, so can animal specialists. Half a world away from *Accion Unida,* in Tanzania on the continent of Africa, live the Masai people. For them, cows are everything. Their homes are made of mud and cow dung. Their clothes are made of cowhide. Their food is milk and beef; though they live in the middle of one of the last great game reserves, they eat almost no wild meat. Their wealth and money, their medium of exchange, is cows. Their migrations follow the pasture grass. Their communities are built around the periphery of central cow *kraals.*

In the eyes of some missionaries, the Masai live in physical and spiritual darkness. The windowless dung homes with their single

chimney holes are so smoky that visiting them makes one's eyes
red. The women, trapped in polygamous marriages, smear fat on
their bald heads and think it's beautiful. The men cover themselves
with red mud from head to foot. The people eat almost nothing
but meat and milk, which they sometimes thicken with a spurt of
blood from a living cow's neck. Many have no schools. No decent
health care. No settled communities. No job training to prepare
them for the modern world. What a pitiable group.

But the Masai don't see it that way. Tall, distinctive, aristocratic,
these people are among the proudest in Africa. They are not afraid
to kill a lion single-handedly. They can run for miles. They know
every cow by name, and its ancestry for generations back. They
speak poetically.

One day, for example, a missionary and his Masai colleague
were discussing the word "faith."

"The Masai word you've used is too weak," said the African. "It
just means 'to agree to' something." He went on to explain:

> He said "to believe" like that was similar to a white hunter
> shooting an animal with his gun from a great distance. Only his
> eyes and his fingers took part in the act. We should find another
> word. He said for a man really to believe is like a lion going after
> its prey. His nose and eyes and ears pick up the prey. His legs
> give him the speed to catch it. All the power of his body is
> involved in the terrible death leap and single blow to the neck
> with the front paw, the blow that actually kills. And as the
> animal goes down, the lion envelops it in his arms (Africans
> refer to the front legs of an animal as its arms), pulls it to
> himself, and makes it part of himself. This is the way a lion kills.
> This is the way a man believes. This is what faith is.

> I looked at the elder in silence and amazement. Faith under-
> stood like that would explain why, when my own was gone, I
> ached in every fiber of my being. But my wise old teacher was
> not finished yet.

> "We did not search you out, Padri," he said to me. "We did
> not even want you to come to us. You searched us out. You
> followed us away from your house into the bush, into the
> plains, into the steppes where our cattle are, into the hills
> where we take our cattle for water, into our villages, into our
> homes. You told us of the High God, how we must search for
> him, even leave our land and our people to find him. But we
> have not done this. We have not left our land. We have not

searched for him. He has searched for us. He has searched us out and found us. All the time we think we are the lion. In the end, the lion is God."[4]

Perhaps it is an understatement to say that the Masai speak poetically.

Because cows are so important in Masai culture, one outsider that Masai respect is a veterinarian. So the Christian Veterinary Society sponsors monthly cow clinics in a score of villages. Masai evangelists come, too. They preach in rich Masai rhetoric to the men lounging around:

"When a man looks at a herd of cows" (says the evangelist, for example), "he will recognize that a certain young cow was sired by a bull that belongs to him. No other people may know by looking that that man knows the cow was sired by his bull. And so it is with all of us, we know we have a common father. We know when we see you that you belong to that bull above, the father who made it possible for all of us to be here."[5]

Village elders who never would come to a Christian meeting listen thoughtfully to the evangelists at the cow clinics.

Like agriculturalists, veterinarians and animal husbandrymen may be ambassadors of God's kingdom.

Take Herb Fuqua, an animal expert with Wycliffe Bible Translators. In the South American jungles, nomads used to hunt freely. Now many are settling down. When they do, the game in their immediate environment doesn't last long—soon their region is "hunted out." Herb has begun to "capitalize" these people with cattle.

In 1954 he began experimenting with twenty-five varieties of pasture grass, testing which would best feed cattle when grown in impoverished jungle soils. He spent the next years cross-breeding cattle—and battling flies, worms, and parasites in wounds, and meeting all the challenges of rusty machinery, continual jungle growth creeping into his pastures, breaks in fences, and interminable breeding records.

Finally the day came when he began shipping calves by canoe, raft, and plane to jungle tribes. By 1974, 235 calves had arrived at 41 locations.

"We have tried everything that has been suggested to us," says one Aguaruna, "and raising cattle is the only thing that has brought us remuneration."

Besides providing stock, Wycliffe Bible Translators have also offered tribal people training in the care of horses, cattle, pigs, and goats, as well as in crop cultivation.

In such projects, the long-term involvement of people like Herb Fuqua is essential. Veterinarians who sweep in and out of places may patch up ailing animals, but do they offer lasting help? Or do they instead make people more dependent than ever by undermining their confidence in their old remedies? Visiting veterinarians must think not only about the animals they treat but about the overall environment. For example, might they be contributing to overbreeding, which will destroy pasturelands? When they prescribe, do they take time to learn about local remedies, using available herbs and materials? Or do they prescribe drugs which are unrealistic because no native can afford them consistently? Do they make a point of learning about local sources of nutrients, local diseases, and locally appropriate water-conservation techniques?

They can learn even from people who are nonliterate, who often know volumes about animals and plants. Take, for example, the Philippine Negritos, who supposedly are among the most backward peoples in those islands. Robert Fox provides an amazing description of them:

> Most Negrito men can with ease enumerate the specific or descriptive names of at least 450 plants, 75 birds, most of the snakes, fish, insects, and animals, and of even 20 species of ants. Moreover, each Negrito can give a description of the colors, habits, foods, calls, etc. of all of the animal, insect, and bird life known to him. . . .
> Besides the ordinary sense of smell, and so forth, there seems to be an instinctive sense of the presence of game. . . . They can track a snake by the smell if it has passed within so many hours. They can tell the kind of meat which a person has eaten. They can scent fruits at a distance if the wind is favorable. They can distinguish the clothes of different persons by their smell. To find out if a person is going to be seriously sick, many pygmies claimed that they could prognosticate by the increasing odor arising from the body of the patient.
> To achieve this feat indeed requires a genuinely scientific

attitude, sustained interest, and a desire for knowledge for its own sake. . . .

Sometimes when in doubt [that a person or an animal has passed through a certain area, the Negrito] will place his ear close to the ground and assure himself of what he had first merely surmised. Having assured himself through his senses of the presence of a live object he will then examine the footprint or the tracks and tell pretty accurately the size and kind of animal that had fled, or, in the case of persons, recognize perhaps by the footprint and even tell the amount of load the person carried if he had a load. . . .

Many times I have seen a Negrito, who, when not being certain of the identification of a particular plant, will taste the fruit, smell the leaves, break and examine the stem, comment upon its habitat, and only after all of this pronounce whether he did or did not know the plant.[6]

To learn a delicate ecosystem takes time. To maximize their effectiveness, visiting animal specialists should sit at the feet of resident animal experts—even nonliterates. Each has something to learn from the other.

Like animal husbandrymen, agriculturalists also need to adapt themselves to a new environment. In the pueblo of Taos, New Mexico, a U.S. government agriculturalist ran a successful program—until he introduced early spring plowing. Then he was drummed out of town. The people said he was insane.

The Taos people believe Mother Earth is pregnant in the springtime. During that season they don't drive their wagons to town. They remove the horseshoes from their horses' hooves. They themselves wear soft-soled shoes.

But the agriculturalist was so absorbed in his own specialty that he never noticed how carefully people walked in the springtime. So he dug into pregnant Mother Earth with a long, sharp plow.

That was the end of his influence.[7]

In Laos, during the 1950's, some Western agriculturalists introduced fertilizer to the local farmers. They welcomed it, but they didn't use it, as the experts had planned, to increase their yield. Rather, they calculated how much fertilized land it would take to produce the same amount of rice as they had harvested before. Then they reduced the size of their planting. They used fertilizer to save them work rather than to expand production.[8]

"Why should I grow a bigger crop?" farmers in many countries ask. "It will just mean more relatives descending on me at harvest time."

In Samoa, an American-Samoan couple couldn't get anyone to clear land for a banana plantation, though they offered good wages. Money didn't motivate the Samoans.

When they opened an "agricultural school," they found that no one wanted courses in general science, poultry-raising, and banana-growing. In fact, students wanted something quite different: classes in English and typing.

It was only accidentally that they discovered how to motivate Samoans to clear the land. A delegation came asking for a loan, which they needed to build a new house for their pastor before the annual church convention. Their cold-hearted local store-keeper wouldn't extend credit, they moaned.

"I have no money," said the wise Samoan husband. "But I'll tell you something. My American wife has plenty. But she's a hard woman. She would never loan you the money. On the other hand, she likes bananas. If you would clear a little plantation for her, I'm sure she would pay you five pounds per acre."

In four days, twelve acres of almost impenetrable jungle were cleared.

Where wages left Samoan hearts cold, church-related buildings set them afire.[9] The wise agriculturalist learns from experiences like these.

Sometimes, for example, Westerners introduce tools that do more harm than good in certain environments. In New Guinea, people tried using steel shovels in their potato gardens for a while. Then they went back to using pointed digging sticks. The shovels were too bulky, and they damaged the still unripe potatoes as well as the roots and vines. They didn't suit a culture where people harvest potatoes all year round.[10]

In Afghanistan, farmers tried using scythes instead of their old sickles. With a scythe a man could cover four times as much ground as he could with a sickle in the same amount of time. A capable development team encouraged the use of scythes for four years. But in the end, the people went back to sickles. The scythes shattered a little more of the grain, and for these poor farmers, every handful counted. They were like doctors in countries without blood banks who learn surgical techniques that spill less blood than ours.[11]

In many parts of the world where the development of water resources is essential, Christian organizations have helped communities dig tube wells. These extend about fifteen feet into the ground. When they are capped and connected to a pump, the water remains clean. These wells not only help agriculture: it is estimated that they will reduce the communicable diseases in villages by as much as sixty percent. Each well costs about $150. This is considerably cheaper than shipping in food every other year.

But wells are a mixed blessing. In Africa, too many deep wells have lowered the water table and increased the desert. A current effort by the United Nations to arrest the deterioration of range lands in thirty-seven African and Middle Eastern countries traces this ruin to more wells and irrigation, more veterinarians, and more active marketing of livestock. Even in drought-stricken Somalia, a report recommends not proliferating more water points until range control measures have been adopted. Shallow tube wells may pose problems, too. When the pumps break, as mechanical things inevitably do, many people don't have the faintest idea how to fix them. The pumps rust. And the people have less water than ever.

Faced with such problems, development specialists hunt for "appropriate technology." These are small, simple pieces of equipment. Usually they don't require much expensive fossil fuel.

In 1967, the Intermediate Technology Development Group, Ltd., published its first catalog, *Tools for Progress: A Guide to Small-Scale Equipment for Rural Development.* Since then, similar groups have sprung up in many countries. In the United States, Volunteers in Technical Assistance (VITA) draws on the knowledge of 4,500 consultants.

One such organization, the Brace Research Institute of McGill University (BRI), found that the use of cooking fuel accounts for eighty percent of the basic energy needs of a Senegalese village. Here, as in many other parts of the world, what goes under the pot costs more than what goes inside it. BRI has risen to the challenge. Using solar cookers, methane digesters, and windmill pumps, BRI has developed a plan that will meet the water, cooking, and lighting needs of a typical Senegalese village of about five hundred people.

Alternative technology groups emphasize the importance of four things:

- simple designs of equipment
- products that do minimal damage to the environment
- decentralized, regional marketing
- low initial cost per workplace

This last emphasis is called a "labor intensive" approach. It contrasts with the "capital intensive" orientation of industrialized countries, where businesses use labor-saving machinery whenever possible. In a 1962 report prepared for the Indian Planning Commission, Fritz Schumacher discussed this matter, arguing for the "labor intensive" approach in India:

> It requires no lengthy argument to agree that India is "long" in labour and "short" in capital. This means that she requires a level of technology, or "capital investment per workplace," that is likely to be very different from that current in the Western countries, which are "long" in capital and "short" in labour. At present, in India as in all other developing countries, the most primitive exists side by side with the most advanced—an artisan employing five rupees' worth of tools, and workers minding machines worth fifty thousand rupees. But the intermediate industrial technology which would really suit India's conditions does not exist in an articulated form, except perhaps accidentally. . . . If, therefore, it is intended to create millions of jobs in industry, and not just a few hundred thousands, a technology must be evolved which is cheap enough to be accessible to a larger sector of the community than the very rich and can be applied on a mass scale without making altogether excessive demands on the savings and foreign exchange resources of the country. . . .[12]

Since this report was written, India has attempted to encourage labor-intensive businesses. In 1976, for example, excise and sales taxes constituted India's biggest source of revenue. Ordinary taxes on consumer goods totaled twenty-five percent. Yet cottage industries which used no power were exempt from taxes. Businesses which used little power enjoyed correspondingly low taxes. In addition, no big factories were allowed to make certain products, such as matches, soap, and some fabrics. With such encouragement, the cottage textile industry blossomed to employ about ten million people. Handicraft exports were bringing $450 million in foreign exchange into the country annually.

On the other hand, some poor farmers and businessmen overseas have objected, "Don't feed us any more alternative technology! We want standard imports!" Why?

Even though a tractor-drawn weeder imported into Nigeria costs sixty times more than its animal-drawn equivalent offered by alternative technology, people desire the former because it carries more status. Often, too, the standard import is part of a more attractive retail package. The sales information about it may be more colorful. Importers may offer generous credit. Installment assistance, and service and parts for repairs, may be part of the deal. Proponents of alternative technology must learn to be cannier businessmen.

Still another hurdle for agriculturalists is mined with potential explosives: the politics of altruism. Some governments, having grown dependent on Western aid, now neglect developing their own agriculture. In national planning, they don't give agriculture the priority it needs. And a flood of surplus food or supplies from the United States can so depress prices that it drives local farmers or suppliers out of business. The next year, the country has less food than ever.

Like the governments that rule them, people can also become habituated to handouts. Bengalis used to rebuild their houses quickly after disasters. But in 1970 a great cyclone flattened Bangladesh, and mammoth amounts of relief supplies poured in. Much of the Bengalis' incentive to help themselves thus dwindled away. Now, in some regions, they tend to wait for outside aid after calamity strikes.

But there are ways to give without making people dependent. After a disaster, the local people must be encouraged to plan, help finance, and participate in the physical work of rebuilding their own communities. Then charity can become a self-help incentive. In one of the worst famine areas of India, for example, people have been paid in food, through the local Gujarat Christian Agency for Relief, to dig irrigation tanks, deepen wells, and build roads in their own villages.

This approach takes time. It requires knowing the language. And progress isn't made nearly so quickly as it would be if we just went in and reconstructed the community for them. But this approach preserves people's dignity and their confidence that they can find solutions to their own problems in the future.

One more hurdle is population growth. In the eighteenth century, in his *Essay on the Principle of Population,* Thomas Malthus introduced this idea. The more food we produce, he warned, the more the population will outstrip it. There is no way there will ever be enough food. Today we know that excessive use of our natural resources is damaging the earth's fragile ecosystem. Pastures are overgrazed. Woods are deforested. Soils are eroded. Air and water are polluted. There doesn't seem to be enough room for all of us. "Lifeboat ethics" argues that if we try to cram many more into the boat, we will all sink. It's better to leave some in the water.

Why do people in poor countries keep having such big families? we wonder. Why don't they start producing more food, and fewer babies? But, as Art Beals of World Concern has observed,

> How many babies would you have if half of your children died before they reached age five . . . and fifty percent of your remaining children would die before they reached their teen years? How many children would you produce if your children were the only means of support for you and your wife when you reach retirement age? These children that are "too many" are born in countries where there is no social security, no medical insurance, no retirement homes. The children's hands will be the only hands available to guide the plow when father can no longer work. Their hands will be the only hands available to cook simple meals over the open fire, launder the families' clothes in a nearby river, provide nursery care for aged parents.[13]

On the other hand, when people have a more secure economic life, they stop having so many children. Birth rates decline. We see this in countries like the United States, European nations, Japan, Taiwan, Singapore, and Costa Rica. Here farms use machines rather than dozens of laborers. Old-age security comes from the government or employer-sponsored retirement programs. Children, who must be educated for many years, become economic liabilities rather than assets. People voluntarily limit their families. These private decisions are much more effective than government birth-control programs.

To slow down the world's population growth, then, one of the best things we can do is to help poor people develop economically. "The poor you have always with you," Jesus said.

"The poor, yes. The hungry, no," says Al Whittaker, executive director of the International Institute of Development. "And there is a world of difference. Typically, in a developing country, there are the relatively few at the top with most of the wealth, the great masses at the bottom with little wealth, and no middle class. So you could improve the economic lot of many by 100 per cent and they would still be poor."[14]

In fact, Jesus was quoting Deuteronomy 15, which continues, ". . . the poor will never cease to be in the land; *therefore* I command you saying, 'You shall freely open your hand. . . .'"

What better way to open our hand than by helping people feed themselves?

---

1. Juan Flavier, *Doctor to the Barrios* (Quezon City, the Philippines: New Day Publishers, 1970), pp. 45-51.

2. "Grain Becomes a Weapon," *Time*, Jan. 21, 1980, pp. 12-22.

3. Bob Owen and David Howard, *The Victor: The Victor Landero Story* (Old Tappan, N.J.: Revell, 1979), p. 134.

4. Vincent Donovan, *Christianity Rediscovered: An Epistle from the Masai* (Notre Dame, Ind.: Fides/Claretian, 1978), p. 63.

5. Mary Peterson, "Veterinarian Reaching Masai through Cattle," *Christian Veterinary Mission Newsletter*, Dec. 1980, pp. 1-3.

6. Robert Fox, "Pinatuba Negrito: Their Useful Plants and Material Culture," *Philippine Journal of Science*, Special Issue, Vol. 81, 1952.

7. Louis Luzbetak, *The Church and Cultures: An Applied Anthropology for the Religious Worker* (Techny, Ill.: Divine Word Publications, 1963), p. 152.

8. William Smalley, "The Gospel and the Cultures of Laos," in *Readings in Missionary Anthropology*, Vol. II, ed. William Smalley (Pasadena, Calif.: William Carey Library, 1978), p. 200.

9. Fay Calkins, *My Samoan Chief* (Honolulu: University of Hawaii Press, 1971), pp. 109-111.

10. Luzbetak, *The Church and Cultures*, p. 200.

11. Paul Johnson in Arthur Simon's *Bread for the World* (Grand Rapids, Mich.: Eerdmans, 1975), p. 61.

12. Fritz Schumacher, "Reflections on the Problem of Bringing Industry to Rural Areas" (New Delhi: Indian Planning Commission, 1962).

13. Arthur Beals, "Dear Mr. Harvey . . . : An Open Letter to Paul Harvey," *World Concern Update*, Feb. 1980, p. 6.

14. Alfred Whittaker, "Saying 'God Loves You' to a Starving Man," Interview in *Christianity Today*, April 1977, p. 20.

CHAPTER 3

BUSINESS
Helping People Support Themselves

"WHY get off welfare if a job doesn't pay much better?" Jim shrugged.

"Listen, brother, we're not going to give you one more red cent. You take the next job that comes along, even if it's for a paperboy."

The job counselor at Christ Church of Northgate in Seattle was laying it on the line. For seven months Jim had been out of work. Christ Church had channeled him to three or four employment interviews, but he wasn't interested.

Surprisingly, however, after this ultimatum, Jim took the next job that became available—though it didn't even pay the minimum wage. Five weeks later, the church was able to place him in a six-dollar-per-hour position.

Why did the church counselor have so much clout? Because he was part of an overall financial advisory service that Jim knew he needed.

At Christ Church, loving your brother means helping him wherever he has trouble. Thus the financial aid program. Yes, there's a food bank for immediate needs. The local Safeway donates "seconds" of staples and other items—rice, beans, flour, mayonnaise, fruits, and cheese.

But this palliative stopgap isn't enough. People need more than food—they need the opportunity to earn food. So the financial advisory program at Christ Church includes regular appointments with budget counselors, small group support, job-training seminars, and job placement.

The church sponsors the job-training seminars about twice a year. Here practical questions—what to expect in an interview, how to write a resume, tips on personal appearance—are set in a scriptural context. God is righteous and orderly. So instead of stealing time or materials or spoiling the quality of his work with sloppy habits, the employee must give a full day's work, seeking the success of his employer, "working as unto the Lord." Such teaching pays off: some employers call the church before advertising a job elsewhere.

With unemployment increasing in the United States, we need programs like the job counseling service at Christ Church. We know how demoralizing extended "breaktime" can be.

But it's worse overseas. In Pakistan, for example, it was estimated that during the 1960's, twenty-three percent of the men in Karachi with ten years of education were unemployed. By 1973, possibly as many as twenty thousand science graduates with university degrees in Pakistan were jobless.

Agricultural aid helps farmers. But all the tools and hybrid seeds in the world won't help a man who has no land. He needs a job.

Consider, for example, the prospects open to Abu in Bangladesh. Nineteen is an age of promise—but not for Abu. Two years ago he discovered that the skin irritation he'd been scratching absentmindedly was leprosy. His future dissolved. Friends and neighbors became distant. He envisioned himself with a black hole for a nose and stumps for fingers. There would be no girls for him. The dreams of nineteen froze.

Abu was luckier than some. He gathered the shattered pieces of his self-image together and hiked to a mission hospital. Sulfone drugs took the offensive. It looks like Abu will keep his fingers and nose, after all.

But what of his future? Former job contacts have written him off. As it is, Bangladesh is no jobhunters' heaven. It is instead the dumping ground of the rivers of India, Nepal, and Bhutan. Every year they rush in torrents through Bangladesh's flood plain. Cyclones from the Bay of Bengal come smashing through regularly. Nearly all the arable land is already under cultivation. There is no place for Bangladesh's population of ninety-three million, expanding at the rate of three percent per year, to go.

A bloody civil war in 1971 tore up the roots of many. Between one and three million people were massacred or died of disease and starvation. A quarter of a million women were raped. Today they and their illegitimate children are adrift: no one will marry them, and their families won't take them back. One quarter of the children in Bangladesh die before their fifth birthday.

Economic problems complicate matters. The sale of jute prod-

ucts accounted for eighty percent of the export earnings in the
1970's. But periodically the jute market collapses. Today, with a
per-capita income of about seventy dollars, Bangladesh is one of
the poorest countries in the world. Many of its people have grown
steadily poorer since World War II. Unemployment and under-
employment are rated at about thirty-seven percent.

Where can Abu find a job? His leprosy may be under control,
but is that enough? Must he spend the rest of his life at the hospital, begging for scraps of food?

Medical care meets Abu's immediate need. But our help is
superficial if we patch a man up and toss him back into an environment where he will starve.

To God's glory, Christians gave Abu a marketable skill.

In the early 1970's, on the tail winds of a cyclone, several
groups joined to form HEED Bangladesh. HEED's aims were to
make improvements in health and agriculture, to help develop
community organization and cottage industries.

What could HEED do for Abu? Wood-block printing looked like
a job possibility. Because this printing is what patterns the fabric
that the poor use for their saris, there is a steady demand for the
skill. HEED persuaded a skilled village craftsman to take on Abu
and another man (also a leper) as apprentices. For twelve months,
Abu and a friend experimented with designs, dyes, and fabrics.
Then, back at the leprosarium, they became teachers. As a result,
napkins, tablecloths, mats, shoulder bags, bedspreads, clothes, and
curtains are now printed with the creative visions of leper patients
whom the medical staff has okayed for the work. In 1980, thirty
thousand pieces were designed. Eager buyers snapped them up.

"You have given my son hope," Abu's mother says as she brings
gifts of vegetables to the HEED staff. "You Christians have done it."
This is the biggest payoff. The lepers who have become craftsmen
have changed radically. Their lives are no longer dead ends.

Reaching out to other groups who have been pushed aside,
HEED has offered them a push toward self-sufficiency. Take the
Indian community as an example. Several generations ago Indians
were imported as indentured laborers to work the tea estates of
East Bangladesh. By now there are more Indians than jobs. But in
this country which fought a bloody war with India in 1947 and
erupted in an anti-Indian coup as recently as 1981, in this nation

where unemployment runs at over thirty percent, finding a job is particularly difficult work for an Indian.

Again the HEED staff stepped in. "What natural resources exist near the tea estates?" they asked.

Everywhere groves of bamboo trees creak gently in the wind, they found. And wild cane sprouts profusely. So HEED trained Lal, a local young man, to make baskets and furniture out of bamboo and cane. Now Lal runs a training center. But not only did Lal learn a saleable skill during his apprenticeship. He also became a Christian. Today, besides working at his job, Lal conducts literacy classes on his own for his people.

No specific project is so important as the process of learning how to tackle problems. Development planners know this. But how can this process be started for people too poor to take risks? Malnutrition and recurring disasters breed apathy, inertia, and suspicion among the poorest of the poor.

On the other hand, if people become independent, if they can support themselves, HEED finds, then they often will take the initiative to meet other personal needs—their own health and educational needs, for example.

Hiring is one of the best "cups of cold water" we can hand to the jobless. But hiring is a tall order. It means skill training. Marketing networks. Raw materials. Tools and equipment. Capital. Red tape. Regular feedback about changing market conditions. If producers don't know how to handle these problems, they will be sheep among wolves.

Marketing means quality control. HEED had to send Manipuri weavings back to their makers several times before they got cloth that would sell. The Manipuris had been robbed by their Muslim neighbors during the war of independence, and HEED wanted to help them. For centuries Manipuri women have woven on backstrap looms. Why not market bedspreads and tablemats? But the first batch were as garish as Joseph's coat of many colors.

In the second batch, the patterns varied alarmingly.

In the third batch, the threads were crooked.

Eventually most of the Manipuri women gave up. "It's too hard," they said. Only three women were willing to keep trying, practicing quietly in their spare time.

Today, now that they see the good money the three persistent weavers are pulling in, many women want to join the program.

HEED's service center in Dacca is the hub of quality-control maintenance as well as of design experimentation, market analysis, and packaging. It even has an art gallery. The service center also gives advice on raw materials. Take, for instance, the wool used in carpets. In Bangladesh, shepherds don't shear their sheep. Tanneries just scrape wool off hides and dump it in a pile. Middlemen collect it and hoard it until the rainy season. Then, because little wool is available, they charge high prices. HEED teaches rugmakers to gather wool in advance, directly from tannery piles.

Beyond locating raw materials, supplying equipment may be one of the most valuable contributions we can make. Worldcrafts in Seattle has given looms to rugmakers in Nepal and Pakistan. After war raged for seventeen years across the Sudan, Christians from several nations did not merely dole out relief. They "recapitalized" forty-seven Sudanese villages with grinding mills, provided farm implements, and helped tailors and blacksmiths get back into business; they also set up training schools. United Action in Colombia shows craftsmen how they can build their own equipment.

But equipment must be supportable. Around the globe, tractors sit unused, rusting, because no one can afford fuel or replacement parts for them. Businessmen equip their offices with electric typewriters and computers—and then go crazy when the power blacks out every other day. We must consider a number of factors to develop equipment wisely. How appropriate is the technology we plan? Can replacement parts be gotten within the country? Is the equipment fuel-efficient, using fuel that is available locally?

At the end of the line, craftsmen need buyers. Christian importers like Jubilee Crafts, Tearcraft, and Worldcrafts tap into sales outlets in the West. England's Oxfam supplies several hundred shops with crafts from poor countries.

On a recent trip, I was looking for some gifts to take home. "Baskets. Or shellwork. Would we have time to shop for some on our way to lunch?" I asked my hostess.

"I know just the place," she smiled. "Not an impersonal touristy store. A couple of my friends overseas have set up a workshop for Capiz shellwork. They've been able to provide jobs for twenty people. The work is beautiful. You'll see."

When she took me to the shop that sold their products, I did see.

When we buy birthday or wedding presents, why not patronize

a store that imports from groups that benefit workers in poor countries? Then our purchases will bless not only the ones who receive them but also the ones who make them. Like Abu and Lal.

It is true that for the middlemen, importing can sometimes be a headache. Not long ago, for example, Worldcrafts sent a check to a group of leather workers in Nepal. But banks in Katmandu had never heard of the Rainier Bank, on which the check was drawn. They sent it back.

"Try a bank draft," advised the Worldcrafts director.

But the company accountant for Worldcrafts had never heard of a bank draft, so he put the request aside. When the draft finally got underway, the American bank involved advised Worldcrafts that Nepal doesn't receive drafts.

So Worldcrafts cabled the money. Fortunately, they also sent a letter. The cable never has arrived. Meanwhile, Worldcrafts has learned that Nepal *does* in fact receive bank drafts.

Importing isn't all fun.

It does, however, allow people the dignity of supporting themselves. Fifty thousand women have been employed in one jute-craft project in Bangladesh. Such craftspeople work creatively, making whole items individually. They use local natural resources which might otherwise go to waste. They use little fuel. By marketing overseas, they bring valuable foreign exchange into their country.

On the other hand, crafts provide only a supplementary income for most, not a dependable steady job for a lifetime. And to insure high quality, continuity of production, prompt delivery, and adaptability to changing market tastes, many evangelical groups sponsoring craft projects employ white foreigners to control them. While local people may have the dignity of supporting themselves, they are not allowed the dignity of controlling their own business.

There are other objections to the craft export business. How much should we encourage poor people to depend on a tourist-type market? This year the craftsmen employed by one Asian exporter are weaving pink-and-purple straw purses—because that's what market research indicates is selling in Florida and California.

There's nothing intrinsically wrong with developing new styles. Take Bali, for instance. In recent years, many Balinese villages independently have reorganized their production of art objects in response to an expanded foreign market. Before 1969, for example, no woodcarving was done in the village of Ketewel. Since then, however, quite a few Ketewel people have studied at government woodcarving schools. By 1976, they had learned enough to renovate their own famous temple. Formerly they had had to employ outsiders for this task.

Change is inevitable. But in the middle of change, the Balinese are retaining certain time-honored patterns as they continue one of the world's great and distinctive artistic traditions. The pink-and-purple purses may be in quite a different category. Does this "art" mirror an authentic aspect of an integrated culture? Or is it an increasingly trivialized response to capricious foreign tastes?

As American buyers, we must also be judicious. How much of our income should we spend on imported plant hangers, tablecloths, and wooden bowls? Do we need to redecorate our homes every year?

Handicrafts that maintain continuity with a rooted tradition are expensive if made by American Indians. As wages rise in Africa, Asia, and Latin America—as we hope they will—their exported crafts will become proportionately costly. Perhaps eventually these crafts, like Rembrandts and giraffes, will be seen only on public display. Few people will be able to support themselves with crafts then.

Madison-Avenue-designed African statues made on assembly lines—of what value are these trinkets? If the working conditions are decent and the wages are fair, creating these statues may be a pleasurable exercise for their makers and a visual joy for their owners. But their purported heritage is sham, and too often results in trivializing the art. We are left with the Muzak of handicrafts.

Marxists charge that capitalist economies pour too much energy into the production and marketing of luxuries, while leaving basic needs unmet. When we consider what some regions lack—when many countries cannot even manufacture paper but must import it, for example—is it right to devote all of the business acumen of our missionaries to the creation of luxury goods for Westerners? Or could we instead help people manufacture locally needed products through full-time rather than supplementary jobs?

That's what the Society for Community Development in Gujranwala, Pakistan, aims to do.

For a vacationer, Pakistan can be breathtaking. The muezzin's call to prayer floats from the minarets in the early dawn. Gathering light bathes the 62-foot-high central ivory dome of the Imperial Mosque in Lahore. White pavilions shimmer in the Shalimar Gardens created by Emperor Shah Jahan. Fine mozaics and calligraphy soar up the walls of monuments inspired by the Mogul conqueror Babur.

But being a Christian in Pakistan may be breathtaking in quite a different sense: it may mean cleaning up other people's urine and bowel movements for the rest of one's life.

At the end of the nineteenth century, hundreds of villagers in the Pakistan Punjab turned to Christ. Most of the Christians in Pakistan today are their children. As it happens, the people caught up in this great movement of the Spirit of God came from the bottom of the Hindu caste system. In the rural Punjab, they worked as farm laborers. Because their caste designated them to do the dirty work, other people steered clear of them. Nobody else would eat with them or sit near them—much less let one of his children marry one of theirs. Or offer one of their children a better job.

In Jesus, members of these "depressed castes" found dignity and love. They flocked to church with hope for a better life. Has their hope paid off?

Not exactly. Today, because of continuing prejudice and fierce job competition, a Christian in Pakistan still often finds that his vocation is going to be dealing in human waste. He might empty cesspools with a bucket, pouring the contents into a tank towed by a tractor. Or he might be a latrine-cleaner, in charge of public toilets. Or he might be privately employed by families to tug their toilet boxes out of the compound wall and empty them. Or, if he is skilled, he might be a *kundiman* who unclogs pipes—but is threatened by sewer gas when he crawls beneath the streets to do his work.

His wife and mother will wipe up waste in public streets and private homes. Though Pakistani women are guarded carefully, no one gives it a thought when a Christian "sweeper" woman goes alone into strange houses. Sweepers are more like machines than human beings.

What does a sweeper find when he goes home? Take one in a typical community of four thousand in Karachi, made up primarily of Christians. The wage earner swings open the iron gate in the brick wall the city built to hide the slum that is his home. Behind it are eighteen ochre-colored, three-story tenement houses. A family, with an average of six members, has one room to live in. To reach it, they must walk across everyone else's balconies, stepping over cooking pots. People who are resting must pull in their legs whenever anyone else wants to get by. But these are the lucky ones. Those not so lucky build shacks of wood, tin, or jute between the tenement houses. Such structures are illegal. Often storms blow them away before the government razes them.

This community shares seven toilets and eleven water faucets— for four thousand people. Piles of rubbish mount in every cul-de-sac. Latrines ooze excrement. Streets are fouled by children, goats, chickens, sheep, cows, and dogs. Yet in the evening so many pull beds out into the street to sleep in relative coolness that a person can hardly find space to move.

It is in this environment that people practice choir songs, rehearse Christmas pageants, memorize Scripture, and try to teach their children what it means to be made in the image of God, an object of the love of God, and a light to the Muslims and Hindus around them.

Maybe it's not so bad. All communities need sanitary engineers. Anybody who has changed a few diapers learns wryly to accept the organic cycle that God has generated. But would we tolerate a high-school career counselor who advised our children that the main job opening for Christians was emptying buckets of other people's waste?

The Society for Community Development, an interdenominational organization, offers an alternative. Its members find out what job needs exist in Pakistan. Then they train boys from poor families, especially Christians, for these openings. Every year several hundred older teenagers study skills like drafting, surveying, welding, carpentry, electronics, and machinist skills at SCD's vocational training center. Most students come from illiterate families with more than six children.

Daily small-group Bible studies focus on the New Testament. Chapel services emphasize the Old Testament. Games of volleyball, basketball, and badminton complement study.

This school provides a model for the government and other agencies. There is no other training center in Pakistan quite like it. Other schools produce white-collar graduates who know the theory of engineering but are awkward in practice. The SCD accepts boys with little academic background. It teaches in the Urdu language. Whenever possible, teachers use blueprints and pictorial diagrams rather than wordy textbooks. Students are drilled on practical skills: they spend countless hours in the workshop. As a result, most of SCD's graduates are employable immediately—beyond the world of toilets.

Locating jobs, providing training, and handling placement: if only we had as many missionaries dedicated to this task as to medicine and education.

Hiring the unemployed, as in businesses that export crafts, is a good start. Training them in locally needed skills and placing them in the local economy is better. But still more can be done: enabling poor people to set up businesses and create new jobs for others is best of all.

In a low-key way, SCD does this. During the disastrous floods of 1973, they designed prefabricated concrete housing components, like beams and door and window frames. At its peak an open-air factory employed almost one hundred men. The components they made, easily transported to remote flooded villages, could be erected by semiskilled laborers in a few hours.

In 1976, in an area where SCD had been helping poor villages develop economically, heavy rains created a new river flowing six miles wide and six feet deep through the desert. The water table rose to within twelve inches of the soil surface. Scores of buildings collapsed.

But in Pakistan, wood for rebuilding is scarce. Even conventional bricks are expensive, as George McRobie points out:

A typical modern brick factory in an industrialized country produces about one million bricks a week. For a developing country this technology has several serious drawbacks. It is very expensive, costing upwards of a million pounds in foreign exchange to install, and running costs are high because spare parts, and energy, generally have to be imported.[1]

SCD uses an alternative: low-cost concrete made of soil. Applying twenty tons of pressure to a mixture of ninety percent soil and ten percent cement, they produce relatively waterproof building blocks on site. This kind of concrete is also used to line irrigation canals. If canals are not lined, ninety percent of the water seeps into the sand within half a mile from its source.

Another small business under SCD's wing is the Consulting and Technical Service. This prepares land surveys and building plans and estimates. Yet another business manufactures metal ankle-and-knee joints for leg braces used in orthopedic rehabilitation. SCD furnishes initial financing, accommodation, equipment, administrative services, and technical support on a commercial basis.

The International Institute of Development, Inc., is another evangelical group that nurtures entrepreneurs in poor countries. It was started in 1971 by a group of Christian businessmen in Washington, D.C. IIDI's director is Al Whittaker, who was formerly executive vice-president of the Mennen Company and president of Bristol-Myers International Corporation. These businessmen sensed that many Western Christians would like to help the poor, but they want to put their money where it will work. Projects have to make sense. IIDI locates such projects and links American investors with them.

Poor businessmen need two things: capital and expertise. IIDI helps provide both. They screen proposals for businesses from would-be entrepreneurs. A cannery. A taxi business. A suitcase-manufacturing plant. A lumber mill. During 1980, IIDI screened over one hundred proposals. Fifty-seven were approved or under consideration, and forty-eight of those got underway during the year. About half are food-related businesses. Besides supporting food industry, IIDI also emphasizes alternative technology; there is a plant in Honduras, for example, that manufactures water wheels.

How does IIDI fund these businesses? Once a project is approved, IIDI informs interested American Christians of the opportunity to make a high-risk, low-interest loan. If an entrepreneur can get a loan from a local bank, IIDI encourages that. But most of these poor businessmen don't own enough property to serve as collateral for a loan. And in some countries banks discriminate against Christians.

How are the funds administered? Since its formation in 1971, IIDI has helped indigenous boards in four countries—Colombia, Honduras, Indonesia, and Kenya—to set up their own private voluntary organizations. Capitalized at about $350,000-$500,000, each center now administers from fifty to seventy-five projects through its own revolving fund.

Carlos Hernandez is a development specialist with the IIDI center in Honduras. He burns with the desire to help his people.

After graduating from seminary, Carlos worked with a youth program. In the process he developed administrative and financial skills. Later he spent a year learning business alongside an American IIDI consultant. Now, besides preaching every other Sunday, Carlos teaches accounting, management, and business law to small entrepreneurs who apply what they learn in the day-to-day management of their businesses.

With such careful monitoring, fewer than five percent of the projects underway prior to 1980 had failed, even though IIDI loans to "high risks."

Many of the loan recipients are Christian leaders who are being swallowed up by inflation. Carlos Moreno, for example, pastored a church first in Bogata, Colombia, then for six years in Boyaca, then for three years in Pereira. Eventually he moved to Cali to pioneer a church. He soon found that there weren't enough believers to support his family. So he began making and selling spices on the side.

"'At least now I could afford bus fare to get to the various meetings throughout the city where I was to preach,'" he said after two months in the spice business.[2]

But when Moreno tried to expand his business, two banks that supposedly were established to help the small businessman turned down his application. IIDI stepped into the gap with a loan of three thousand dollars. Using this, Moreno got a license to sell nationwide, registered his trademark, built up and expanded his inventory, and bought some equipment.

Today his sales volume averages three thousand dollars a month. He employs twelve people, including another pastor who uses his wages from this job to supplement the small income he receives from his tiny church. Moreno himself has been able to reduce the time he spends on the business: he has cut back to five days a month. The rest of the time he is the executive secretary of the Panamerican Mission, overseeing one hundred churches scattered throughout Colombia.

In fact, IIDI has found that Christian leaders have many of the qualities needed for successful entrepreneurship. And often these businessmen follow Moreno's pattern: after getting on their feet financially, they reduce the hours they devote to business so that they can spend more time doing Christian work.

While some American supporters develop personal partnerships with overseas entrepreneurs through IIDI, others prefer to contribute to the IIDI's revolving fund. Many of these contributions are matched by AID and the Overseas Private Investment Corporation, a small U.S. government agency organized to encourage investment in small businesses in developing countries. All of this helps fund IIDI's work. The average project receives seven thousand dollars from the U.S. side. A twelve percent interest rate is not uncommon.

Margaret King, eighty-one, is one of IIDI's partners. Recently she invested $1,500 of her retirement money to help a poor Colombian baker. "'I've long had the feeling that a good deal of help for the poor gets lost in the pockets of public officials,'" says this retired schoolteacher. "'Somehow it never gets to the people it's meant for. And although as a Christian I wanted to be sensitive to people's needs, I wasn't about to trust a system that wouldn't get the money where I wanted it to go.'"

IIDI's approach attracted her. "'When I heard about a way that I could loan some money to a family in Colombia starting their own business, it sounded so logical,'" she remembers. "'In fact, I've since taken on another project in Indonesia, financing a small tractor for a group of farmers who needed one and couldn't get a local loan. They'll both pay me back by the time I need the money—and in the meantime, they'll have gotten on their feet.'"[3]

Often we Christians would rather get involved in medicine or teaching than in business. The way we see it, work in health and education is philanthropic; participation in business is greedy. And businessmen, especially overseas, have to dirty their hands with all sorts of ethical dilemmas. Some of the chapter titles in Wally Armbruster's book, *It's Still Lion Versus Christian in the Corporate Arena,* tell the story:

- Keeping the Sabbath Day Holy versus Keeping it Profitable
- Loving Each Other as I Have Loved You versus the Law of Supply and Demand
- Thou Shalt not Kill versus the Competitive Spirit
- Thou Shalt not Steal versus Knowing a Perq When You See One
- Thou Shalt not Covet versus Increasing Your Share of the Market

Cutthroat competition, partial truth in advertising, using people as things, bribery, covetousness, aggressiveness, looking out for number one, driving out high-quality art with meaningless repro-ductions, replacing holistic lifestyles with compartmentalizing jobs, stripping lands of natural resources, polluting the environ-ment, materialism—who wants to struggle with all these problems? We forget that managing physical resources creatively is as much a part of God's world as is healing or teaching. According to R. Hooykaas,

> Even before the Fall man had "to dress and to keep" the garden of Eden; after the Fall it was the fatigue of labour, not labour itself, which was the punishment. The biblical authors do not praise *otium* (leisure). . . .
>
> Jewish rabbis had to learn a trade. Jesus was a carpenter, and the son of a carpenter, and Paul asked the Thessalonians to work with their hands, as he had given the example himself; by "his occupation he was a tentmaker. . . ."
>
> In the Bible all labour is considered holy to the Lord. . . . Occupation with material things, which are, no less than im-material things, God's creatures, is not thought to be dishonour-able. God Himself created all visible and invisible things. . . . In the Bible, the craftsman is honoured and therefore so too is manual work.[4]

But it is true that businessmen slog through ethical quagmires. Possibly this happens because business means money, and money means power. At any rate, sometimes businessmen get sucked into the mire. Eli Black, for example, was president of United Brands, the biggest banana producers in the world. A godly Jew, Black immersed himself in Scripture every Sabbath, and it charged his life with goodness. He raised the wages of his Central American farm workers to six times those of his competitors. He upgraded workers' housing, wired in free electricity, and gave them housing alternatives. He did all this even though his advisors told him that market conditions didn't dictate that he provide any of these benefits. His lettuce subsidiary was the first grower to settle with the United Farm Workers' union headed by Cesar Chavez. He often gave money to employees who had family or business problems.

Nineteen seventy-four hit United Brands below the belt. Banana taxes of $11 million were levied by Latin American countries in the fall quarter. Hurricane Fifi damaged 20 million dollars' worth of company property in Honduras. The cost of cattle feed went up; one subsidiary selling cattle lost $40 million.

In February 1975, Black smashed his office window with his briefcase, and fell forty-four stories to his death. Later it was revealed that he had agreed to offer a Latin American official $2.5 million to roll back the banana tax by fifty percent.[5]

Sometimes the quagmire wins. But just because the business world is difficult doesn't mean we have the right to refuse to deal with it. Avoiding the problem of poverty won't make it disappear for those who must suffer it. Soothing our consciences with charity is not enough. And agricultural aid is not enough: what helps poor farmers may push both peasant sharecroppers and urbanites comparatively further down the economic scale. Eventually they may turn in desperation to violence.

"Crime doesn't pay," we say. But what does?

We can be part of the answer. We can set up sheltered workshops that make crafts to export, like HEED does. We can train people in locally needed skills and place them in the local economy, like SCD does. We can provide capital and expertise so that they can set up their own businesses and create jobs for others, like IIDI does.

---

1. George McRobie, *Small Is Possible* (New York: Harper & Row, 1981), p. 42.

2. Carlos Moreno, quoted in Dean Merrill's "The Spice Maker," Full Gospel Business Men's Fellowship *Voice*, July-Aug. 1980.

3. Margaret King, quoted in Dean Merrill's "A New Way to Help the Third World," *Christian Herald*, Jan. 1980.

4. R. Hooykaas, *Religion and the Rise of Modern Science* (Grand Rapids, Mich.: Eerdmans, 1972), pp. 83-84.

5. Oliver Williams, "The Eli Black Story," Case Study Institute, University of Notre Dame, Notre Dame, Ind., 1978, quoted in Oliver Williams' and John Houck's *Full Value: Cases in Christian Business Ethics* (San Francisco: Harper & Row, 1978), pp. 141-146.

CHAPTER 4

POLITICS
Helping People Fight Oppression

HELPING people in developing countries grow more food is basic. But right now enough grain is produced to supply every person in the world with three thousand calories a day. That is approximately the daily caloric intake of the average American.[1]

Production is not the root problem. It's the food distribution system that has broken down. Arthur Beals provides some of the sad facts:

- Did you know that the "food poor" countries export two dollars' worth of food to the "food rich" countries for every dollar's worth of food they import from us?
- AFRICA is a net exporter of barley, beans, peanuts, fresh vegetables and cattle, yet it has a higher incidence of protein-calorie malnutrition among young children than any other continent.
- MEXICO now supplies the United States with over one-half of its supply of several winter and early spring vegetables, while infant deaths associated with poor nutrition are common.
- Half of CENTRAL AMERICA'S agricultural land produces food for EXPORT, while in several of its countries the poorest 50 per cent of the population eat only half the necessary protein.
- HAITI, the hungriest country in the Western Hemisphere, with 25 per cent of its children severely malnourished, is a prime supplier of beef for one of America's favorite burger chains.[2]

Every year since 1955, rich, developed nations like the United States have imported approximately twice as many dollars' worth of food from poor countries as we have exported to them— because we can afford to pay for the food, and parents of starving children can't.[3] According to Beals,

The problem of hunger is a problem of distribution. Poor hungry countries must sell their food supplies to pay interest charges on development loans to rich, industrialized countries. They must export desperately-needed food in order to earn dollars to purchase oil to keep their power plants and small industries operating. Otherwise, there will be no jobs for those who live in cities.

The problem of hunger is a problem of power. The powerful elite of our world make decisions to use the world's resources to enrich 25 per cent of the world's people while the 75 per cent of our world who are important producers just don't have the political or economic power to compete.[4]

Beneath this inequality smolders a volcano. José Miguez Bonino writes,

> It is not only that a sixteen-year-old Latin American of this land weighs ninety-five pounds and is five feet tall; the point is that at the other side of the avenue he can see other boys the same age who are six feet six and weigh one hundred and twenty-six pounds. It is not just that they will hardly live to see their grandchildren, their life expectancy being way below forty. They know that disease and death can be pushed back and the joys of life can be enjoyed twenty years more. Rapid and luxurious cars, TV sets, new dresses, fun and comfort are displayed everywhere, and even backwoods populations can see them in the newspapers in which their miserable purchases are wrapped. Commercials and political propaganda, Sears Roebuck catalogues and Communist pamphlets produce the same results. The eyes of the poor are transfixed by the picture of this heaven he must obtain at all costs. Life without it is intolerable. This is the revolutionary temper, this is the face of the Latin American and of the whole underdeveloped world—a face contorted by hunger, expectation and wrath. This is the face of revolutionary man.[5]

For at least thirty years, international agencies have promoted a "war on hunger" through technical modernization. The use of better techniques. Fertilizer. Pesticides. Equipment. New seeds.

The theory was that subsistence farmers would produce and sell a surplus. Cash income would enable the peasant farm family to break out of the cycle of poverty. More available food would mean that even city people would eat better. More food sold abroad would bring in desperately needed foreign exchange.

But in many places the war on hunger has widened the gap between rich and poor. While more food per person has been grown, proportionately more people now go hungry. Why?

First, no amount of modern techniques can make a prosperous farmer out of somebody who doesn't own land. And a great proportion of the poor in developing countries are landless laborers, urban or rural.

Second, in societies where big differences separate the powerful and the poor, the powerful will corner the market on any helpful information or products offered by aid agencies. They will emerge from the program better off than ever—leaving the poor in comparatively greater squalor.

Take the "Green Revolution." In both India and the Philippines, grain production increased dramatically in the 1970's because of this package of technical advances. Yet in India, although food production outstripped population growth, people ate less grain per capita in 1977 than they had in 1960. In Thanjavar, India, for example, rice yields have been three times the national average. But the landless laborers who harvest the rice stay alive by eating the rats that live on the mountains of stored surplus rice.[6] In the Philippines, rice production almost doubled during the 1970's. Yet in the last years of the decade, Filipinos ate less rice than any other Asians.

A major Philippine credit scheme for small farmers is called Masagana 99, a program funded by AID. To participate in Masagana 99, a farmer must use only certain seeds, which require massive doses of fertilizer and pesticide. Who sells these products? A company called Planters Products, Inc., reportedly owned by cronies of President Marcos. For many small farmers, the costs of these products have been greater than the benefits. Incidentally, under this program rural banks were allowed to borrow money from the Central Bank at one percent per year and loan it to poor people at a hundred percent per year. Within two years after Masagana 99 began, the rural banking system had doubled its gross income. But hundreds of farmers had lost their land when natural calamities left them unable to repay their credit loans.[7]

Hunger can grow worse when it is approached as only a technical problem. Reducing hunger means readjusting political and economic systems to better distribute opportunities.

Juan Perez Alfonzo, a Venezuelan who has been called the

father of OPEC, went to his death bitterly disappointed at the way the influx of oil money had increased the gap between the rich and the poor in his country.

"'Oil money has done nothing but lead us to waste,'" he told reporters in 1978. "'This oil income, from the very beginning, has been hurting us. If oil were to disappear, it might be better for us. . . .

"'One cannot plant oil. It is impossible. Our solution does not lie in imitating the United States, in trying to send rockets to the moon.

"'We must try to produce enough black beans to feed the Venezuelans. For this, we do not need capital. We need devotion and we don't have devotion because of all that money.

"'When you receive so much dung from the devil, you can do nothing but wallow in it.'"[8]

Pouring money into a country for the powerful and well-organized to control doesn't help the hungry very much.

But what can we do? If the elite of Venezuela or the Philippines corner all the profits, we can hardly send in the Marines to set things right!

We must not wash our hands of this matter too soon, though. What can we do? First, in the missions projects we support, we can go beyond medicine and agriculture. We can support projects that help poor people own their land and businesses. We can support their struggle for increasing control of the political processes that dominate them.

Take the Bangladesh Rural Advancement Committee, as described by the Institute for Food and Development Policy. This group is supported by Oxfam-America.

In one village where BRAC has been working, forty percent of the two thousand people were landless. Two percent of the population were rich landowners. But fallow, vacant land lay all around. It was the abandoned property of those who had fled to India during the 1971 war of liberation—now government land. Rich landowners used it for illegal grazing or cultivation.

BRAC taught the people to read. It did so through discussions of real problems facing village Bengalis. Armed with a new skill and with better articulated ideas about their situation, the poor people of this village formed the Rajhasan Landless Cooperative

Society. They started petitioning the government to grant them title to some of the abandoned land.

Two years later, after unrelenting corporate pressure from the cooperative, the government ceded them sixty acres. This amounted to one-and-one-half acres per family.

Then the local hassles started. The rich landowners were alarmed because they were losing their illegal use of the once-abandoned land. And they were losing their stranglehold on the poor laborers. They incited other villagers to break the irrigation canal on which the cooperative's land depended. They tried to keep the cooperative from using the river. But they didn't try too hard, because they suspected that starting from scratch would prove too difficult for farmers with little land and no tools or capital.

"They'll be mortgaging their farms right back to us. Give them one season," they laughed to each other.

Instead, the new farmers got a loan for equipment from BRAC at twelve percent interest instead of the fifty to two hundred percent rate available from local moneylenders.

At the end of the first season, in spite of the bad harvest weather, the new farmers paid back the loan, plus interest. Now the members of the cooperative want to extend their joint activities to fishing. And they are feeling adventuresome enough to take the initiative in seeking better health care and child care. Rather than being passive recipients, they are even going out of their way to seek out family-planning information.[9]

What can we do? We can support projects that will build new political and social structures, aimed at giving people more control over the distribution of their economic resources.

Consider the Leme Movement in northern Brazil. Here poor fishermen sell their catch to wholesalers, then stand by and watch the middlemen sell the same fish for twice as much. If they rent rafts, they must pay the owners fifty percent of their profits. During the summer they make fifty dollars a month; during the rainy season they make one dollar a month. Their treadmill existence involves fishing, selling, playing dominos, getting drunk, eating, sleeping, fishing. . . . Yet, superstitiously and fatalistically, they shrug, "God wants it that way."

Father Alfredo Schnuettgen, a Franciscan priest, came to northern Brazil. For five months he sat on the beach, talking and listening to these fishermen. At the end of that time he could not say he had made a single friend. Yet he was trying to apply the new directives of the Second Vatican Council: listen to the people and learn from them. So he stayed.

Rather than giving to these poor fishermen, Schnuettgen challenged them to give. He prodded them to aid the sick and the elderly in their own community. It was his Christian appeal to their consciences that punctured their fatalism. When the rainy season began this time, they came to the priest, troubled. "Now, Father, what about the sick and elderly? And what about us, for that matter?"

Schnuettgen helped them form a cooperative. Eventually they got credit from a local merchant, primarily because the priest stood beside them. They bought wood and built seven rafts. At great sacrifice, they paid off the debt without coming to Schnuettgen for more help. Later Schnuettgen secured a loan from a European church to build an ice locker for fish storage. Finally able to preserve their catch, they no longer had to use the wholesalers, and they were able to lower their prices. Sales boomed.

Throughout, it was a struggle. Their first common fund was exhausted in a month. Their fish-stall manager and his family went almost unnourished during the rainy season, profits were so small. The day after they erected their ice locker, a wild storm swept both hut and locker away. And the members quarreled violently. Their long fish-knives were always close at hand. Some would come to the headquarters half-drunk, looking for loans. Others would shirk their share of the work.

Nevertheless, the Leme Movement of Christian communities grew out of this struggle. It includes about 350 fishermen's families scattered up and down the coast. They organize Christian teaching as well as economic projects.[10]

Today, in thousands of squalid Roman Catholic parishes throughout Latin America, "base communities" somewhat like the Leme Movement shine as lights in a dark place, spreading the good news of the Gospel and of economic development through cooperation.

Cooperatives are no panacea, however. In many cases they are economic disasters. Too often these failures follow imported models of social organization. Too often we have not taken time to learn whether there are credit association patterns which are indigenous. Yet in many parts of South and East Asia, Latin America, and Africa, such associations constitute time-honored investment banks. Some immigrants to the United States have brought this kind of financial arrangement with them. In Seattle, for example, where in 1920 almost fifty percent of the hotels were owned by Japanese, most were financed by a credit association known as *tanomoshi.*

An alternative to cooperatives, which nevertheless acknowledges the group rather than the isolated individual, was developed by Don Richardson when he capitalized small shops in New Guinea with thirty-five dollars' worth of goods each.

Richardson gave the same advice to each prospective merchant: "Go to the oldest man in your group and make a deal. Explain why you cannot give away your goods—the village soon would not have a store. Then ask him if you can refer to him all the relatives and friends who come asking for free goods. He can explain the situation to them. The refusal will be firm but indirect. And you promise that at the end of the year, as a token of gratitude, you will give the elder a shiny new ax."

This plan has worked. Businesses in other countries have successfully employed a similar tactic: they have reduced absenteeism by visiting their employees' home regions and explaining to family elders why coming to work faithfully and punctually is essential.

What can we do? We can put our support behind such projects as the Leme Movement, or the BRAC community development approach. In evaluating these programs, we may be helped by a list of questions developed by the Institute for Food and Development Policy:

Ten Questions to Ask About a Development Project
1. Whose project is it? Is it the donor agency's? or
   Does it originate with the people involved?
2. Does the project define the problem to be tackled as a technical or physical deficiency (e.g., poor farming methods or depleted soils) that can be overcome with the right technique and skills? or
   Does it first address the underlying social, economic and political constraints that stand in the way of solving the physical or technical problem?
3. Does the project strengthen the economic and political position of a certain group, creating a more prosperous

enclave which then becomes resistant to change that might abolish its privileges? or
Does it generate a shift in power to the powerless?
4. Does the project focus only on the needs of individuals? or
Does it help individuals who are now powerless to see their common interest with others who are also exploited, thus leading to unified efforts through which collective strength is built?
5. Does the project merely help individuals adjust to their exploitation by such external forces as the national government or the international market? or
Does it encourage an understanding of that exploitation and a resistance to it?
6. Do new skills and information remain only with the leaders? or
Does the project involve an educational process for all the participants?
7. Does the project, through the intervention of outside experts, take away local initiative? or
Does it generate a process of democratic decisionmaking and a thrust toward self-reliance that can carry over to future projects?
8. Does the project reinforce dependence on outside sources for material and skills? or
Does it call forth local ingenuity, local labor and local materials, and can it be maintained with local skills?
9. Will success only be measured by the achievement of objectives specified at the outset? or
Is the project open-ended, with success measured as the project progresses?
10. Is it a two-way (if possible face-to-face) dialogue in which the recipient also evaluates the donor and they together evaluate the project?[11]

A caution: It is naive to assume a people's movement will be just. Grassroots organizations, too, have their power grabbers who determine to be big ducks even in small ponds. The virtuous "new man" of an egalitarian society is a Leninist myth which does not square at all with our Christian understanding of the nature of man.

Furthermore, Marxists often take over grassroots movements in poor countries. While at first they may cooperate genially with Christians and freethinkers—indeed, that is one of their strategies where Christians turn out to be opinion leaders—in nation after nation there has come a point where Marxists have turned on Christians and others, sold them out, betrayed them, and reverted to a doctrinaire totalitarianism and atheism.

Why does Marxism attract people? Marxists offer a practical program to break out of the cycle of poverty. People come home after spending long hours working in unsafe conditions at a factory, if they are lucky—or from picking up rags and bottles, if they are not—to tin-roofed cardboard shacks perched over sewers. They drift to the largest shack, which boasts a TV. Picking the lice out of each other's hair, they absorb reruns of *Charlie's Angels*. Health. Energy. Waste. The marvel of the U.S. standard of living, made possible by the systematic rape of the raw materials of developing countries, enforced by unequal trade treaties with a local opulent oligarchy. For us, it means fashions, travel, sports; for them, infant mortality, TB, illiteracy. And the ironic awareness that we all are equally human, equally capable of responsibility, choice, and dignity.

Into this imbalance come the Marxists. They are organized, dedicated, and persistent. They can adapt equally well to living comfortably or living primitively. They will teach in the university one year, and retreat to live in the jungle without shoes the next. If they are shot in the right arm, they will learn to write political books with their left hand. They offer a concrete program for change.

If reform movements are to be kept from turning Marxist as a last resort, viable alternatives must exist. Technical development will not be enough. Raising people's consciousness about root problems and local human resources must also play a part.

We have little right to meddle in the internal politics of other nations. But there are three levels of political involvement open to us. One is the national level—and some will argue that foreigners, as guests of the government, should not interfere here.[12] But at a humbler and lowlier level stands the local community. Here, as we have seen in the cases of Bangladesh and Brazil, thoughtful development consultants, who are aware of some of the fundamental causes for continuing poverty, can hardly justify avoiding politics. At the other end of the political spectrum is the international level. Here, too, when we discover how powerful international aid and trade policies are, and how we can in fact influence them, we can hardly excuse uninvolvement.

We Americans are benevolent. Our voluntary charities, like United Way, surprise many visitors from abroad. In 1976, private voluntary foreign aid from the United States totaled $1 billion, and missionary giving probably another $1 billion.[13]

Yet poor nations would far rather have trade than aid. And the two billion we gave in 1976 dwindles when compared with other figures: trade between developing and industrialized nations in 1976 amounted to $200 billion, and foreign investment in developing countries another $46 billion.[14] But what kind of trade is this?

On the positive side, a transnational corporation provides a poor country with capital to form businesses of significant size. It provides thousands of jobs for local people. It imports advanced technology. It provides skill training of many kinds. It injects needed foreign currency—like dollars—into the local economy. It offers incentives for developing a modern world view—efficient, goal-oriented, time-conscious, assertive, and progressive. In some cases, it offers benefits to employees—health, housing, education—at least at the higher management levels.

Illustrating how transnational corporations can enrich a local economy, Singapore is a model studied by many. A sleepy tropical island that became a self-governing state in 1960, Singapore in the intervening years has industrialized so astutely that by 1980 its real growth rate was 10.2 percent. In the period from 1970 to 1980, Singapore's average real growth rate was 9.5 percent. No other nation outside the petroleum-rich countries can boast such expansion. As of 1981, the gross national product per capita was over $5,000. Unemployment is under four percent. Recently Singapore's harbor succeeded Yokahama's as the second-busiest harbor in the world, next to Rotterdam.[15]

Basic necessities like food and housing are available to almost every Singaporean. Seven out of ten families live in government-built high-rises. Some Western visitors find these complexes bleak and cramped. But unlike the design of many U. S. and British high-rise projects, Singapore's apartment design has improved over the years: the buildings show more individuality, and offer greenery, playgrounds, jogging paths, and local "hawker centers." Apartments for the rich stand cheek by jowl with those of the

poor. Extended families are allowed up to four adjacent apartments. Ethnic balance in each complex is assured by the application of a secret quota system in screening applicants. On the debit
side, such ethnic balance can dilute the richness of former ethnic
neighborhoods, such as the Malay *kampongs* sprawling through
urban real estate, which are bulldozed to make room for more
high-rises.

Crime in Singapore has dropped radically. Murderers, kidnap-
pers, and drug offenders are killed. Those guilty of assault receive
long jail sentences. Only police and a few high officials can own
guns; hunters store their weapons at police stations and sign them
out when they want to go shooting. Anyone who litters the streets
is fined the equivalent of $238 in U. S. currency. Government boats
prowl the harbor regularly, on the lookout for tankers that might
be spilling oil.

Singapore's authoritarian prime minister for the past twenty-
four years, Lee Kwan Yew, has directed this development. Since
1979 he has been pressing for a "second industrial revolution,"
and has made Singapore a leading supplier of vitally needed "First
World" products—electronic components, computer hardware,
medical and pharmaceutical products, machine tools. Lee saw
the dangers in Singapore's strong labor-intensive industries in the
1970's. Poor countries might squeeze Singapore out by paying
their workers lower wages. Rich countries might impose tariffs on
Singapore's products in order to protect the jobs of their own
citizens. To move Singapore toward this new industrial revolution,
the National Wages Council has begun handing out annual sets of
guidelines. In 1979, employers had to raise their wage bills by
twenty percent. This gave them strong incentive to buy modern,
automated equipment and to update employee skills. Firms that
complied received radical tax breaks.

Many Singaporeans chafe at some aspects of Lee's Confucian
leadership style—whether at the rules on the length of men's hair
during the 1960's or the severe school exams that channel many
teenagers into technical training instead of college. Nevertheless,
most Singaporeans want to continue to be part of the ten percent
club. To do so in a nation with almost no natural resources, Lee
argues, requires discipline and order.

Transnational corporations can enrich the lives of ordinary
people. In general, Singapore illustrates this. On the negative side,

however, transnational corporations often maintain a stranglehold on small nations, first of all because of their size. They are enormous, as shown by the sampling of sales figures compiled by George Fuller:

> General Motors' 1978 sales totaled $63 billion, Exxon's were $60 billion. Sears, Roebuck sold $18 billion worth of hammers, socks, and other things. For its efforts General Motors showed an income of $3.5 billion; Exxon $2.8 billion; and Sears, Roebuck almost $1 billion. Compare those figures to the 1978 Gross National Product (total of all goods and service produced) for Zimbabwe ($3 billion), or Israel ($15 billion), or Egypt ($16 billion), or South Africa ($38 billion), or Switzerland ($55 billion).[16]

Transnational corporations are huge. Unfortunately, they tend to emphasize easy profits and united military defenses rather than paying good wages, providing safe working conditions, offering profit-sharing plans, increasing ownership of land for the landless, and applying pressure to ensure fair and speedy trials for those arrested for civil protest. Corporations based in "developed" countries tend to press for unequal trade treaties; squeeze out local entrepreneurs, patent-holders, trade unions, and even those attempting to make the nation self-sufficient in food production; and dump unsafe products on foreign markets. They have little motivation to market simple products to the poor, such as a fifty-dollar refrigerator or a one-horsepower motor; instead, they market internationally to global islands of the comfortable.[17]

Consider tariffs, for example. Developing nations cry that we in the West (and Japan) have usurped their raw materials for our industry. So we employ a great number of industrial workers to process these raw materials. If Third World countries processed their own raw materials, their exports would be worth more, and they could offer more and better jobs to their people. But we Americans want to keep as many good-paying jobs as possible, increase the value of our exports, and minimize the cost of our imports. So we impose tariffs on foreign processed goods.

This makes it uneconomical for developing countries to industrialize. The most economical thing for them to do is to sell their raw materials. For some countries, this leads to one-crop plantation

economies where workers have no choice of jobs because there is
only one occupation to "choose."

Then we sell our industrial goods, made from their raw materials, back to them—naturally at a higher cost than their raw
materials—thereby increasing their national debt. Meanwhile, we
advertise heavily to stimulate the felt needs of their elite and
encourage them to buy all our products. In order to do this, the
elite keep more of the nation's wealth for themselves.

Is it any wonder, then, that Latin American theologian Gustavo
Gutierrez explodes,

> Development is now used in a pejorative sense . . . in Latin
> America. . . . One . . . reason . . . is that development . . . has been
> frequently promoted by international organizations closely
> linked to groups and governments which control the world
> economy—in such a way that the rich get richer while the poor
> get proportionately poorer. . . . Developmentalism came to be
> synonymous with reformism and modernization, that is to say,
> synonymous with timid measures, really ineffective in the long
> run and counterproductive to achieving a real transformation.[18]

This feeling is widespread. Many sound Latin American evangelicals squirm when they hear the word *desarrolismo* (development), and refuse to use the term in their own conversation.

But even if we wanted to influence international politics, what
could we do in comparison with a $68-billion-a-year corporation?

George Fuller, Dean of the Faculty at Westminster Seminary, has
written his master's thesis in business administration on the impact the church has on corporations. Evangelicals, he finds, have
tried to affect corporations by moral suasion, boycotts, selective
investment, and shareholder resolutions.

California grapes, Ugandan coffee, J. P. Stevens sheets, Nestle's
chocolate, and sponsors of objectional TV shows all have been
boycotted by Christians in recent years, in efforts to change the
controllers' behavior.

Selective investment has included divestiture: Christians have
gotten rid of stocks in companies that have done something they
find objectionable. Selective investment may also include taking
risks in favor of the poor. According to George Fuller's article
"Making Business Behave," for example, "in 1968 the United
Presbyterian Church directed that its boards and agencies be

authorized to invest 30% of funds not otherwise restricted 'in housing and businesses in low and middle income areas, some of which may offer a low return and higher than normal risk.'"[19]

As for shareholder resolutions, churches and similar groups submitted 111 of these in 1979. Affirmative lending, agribusiness, safeguarding the rights of employees in Coca-Cola's foreign subsidiaries, and many other aspects of transnational corporations were the subjects of such resolutions. According to Fuller, by 1980, "25 (of the 111 resolutions) were successfully negotiated with management, 44 qualified for resubmission at subsequent meetings (by gaining at least three per cent of the vote. . .)."[20]

One corporate shareholder is Anthony Campolo, a sociology professor at Eastern College and a former missionary to the Dominican Republic. In an article entitled "The Greening of Gulf and Western," Campolo describes what he came to believe:

> . . . only a radical restructuring of the economic institutions of the capitalistic world would facilitate the emergence of economic justice and social equality. I was convinced that institutions designed to make profits could not adequately and simultaneously meet human needs. Believing myself to be a God-ordained David, I looked for some corporate Goliath which I could fell with a single shot. I decided my prophetic energies would be directed at the multinational corporation conglomerate, Gulf and Western.[21]

This corporation has vast sugar plantations in the Dominican Republic, where Campolo had seen many children wasted by malnutrition.

Campolo and a few friends bought some shares of stock. That "entitled [them] to go to the stockholders meetings and confront executives and major shareholders with the nature of their sin. . . ."[22] As Campolo explains it,

> We believed GW was God's vineyard and its executives were unfaithful stewards who were oppressing the poor. We believed we were the messengers of God who had come to bring warnings from him, the owner. If these unjust stewards did not listen to us we were prepared to inform them that one day soon the true owner of Gulf and Western would return and he would punish them. In our arrogance, we assumed we were speaking for God and that these executives were enemies of the Almighty.[23]

As events unfolded, GW executives invited Campolo and his friends to discuss matters further in GW's New York offices. There Campolo was told that the plantation soil was too poor for sub- 'sistence farming; it was particularly well-suited for growing sugar cane. He learned also of GW's wage policy and housing and health programs.

What other concrete proposals could Campolo offer?

After doing some research, Campolo suggested investment in a promising agricultural college. GW executives responded imme- diately. They visited the campus, secured a significant grant for it, and plugged the college into their far-flung network of contacts.

On April 30, 1980, A GW officer called Campolo to tell him that the company had just made a commitment to spend up to $100 million for the social and economic benefit of the Dominican Republic.

Campolo still objects to GW's emphasis on tourism, and to the Dominican Republic's one-crop plantation economy. Nevertheless, he now views transnational corporations as powers to be re- deemed. Now, he writes, "I choose to follow the suggestion of Berkhof and view capitalistic institutions as principalities and powers in need of redemption. I believe Romans eight tells us these institutions are 'groaning and in travail waiting for the sons of God' to help them serve the purposes for which they were created."[24]

Jesse Jackson is a Christian leader who seeks economic oppor- tunities for Black Americans. In 1982, Jackson's Operation PUSH successfully influenced the Seven-Up Company to commit itself to spending $61 million to develop Black businesses. Jackson has negotiated similar deals with other major corporations.

Corporations can be influenced. For many of us, shareholder resolutions are a possible means of influence. In the final analysis, George Fuller believes, the power of the shareholder resolution is moral rather than economic. Christians don't have a corner on the market. Yet—Fuller quotes Frank White, director of the Corporate Information Center—"'The real power of the church is in con- sciousness-raising and in embarrassing the corporation into doing what it ought to be doing.'"[25] Fuller continues,

The resolution, according to their view, becomes simply a method for making a moral and ethical statement in the world.

In a recent confrontation between the churches and IBM, the churches' power was not to be measured in the percent of total votes their resolution carried (less than two percent) but in the television coverage of its effort, in the newspaper accounts, in the high visibility of church representation both inside and outside the meeting, and in the resulting impact not only on the company and its management but also on the public.[26]

Fuller concludes, "On the Sunday before writing these words I preached in a church whose annual report showed a fund invested in twenty different corporations. This church is 'conservative': its members would have little interest in the ministry of the Interfaith Center for Corporate Responsibility, seeing it as another 'liberal' cause. But that church owns those companies, for good or for bad. What indeed should the church do?"[27]

Some American Christians, after consulting the research of the Interfaith Center for Corporate Responsibility, lobby transnational corporations who have major offices in our country. Others join Bread for the World, a movement of 30,000 Christian citizens, and lobby our government, asking that justice and mercy be shown in specific bills in Congress.[28]

Some Christians have argued, according to A. N. Triton, that the New Testament's teachings on government—Romans 13:7; 1 Peter 2:13-17—"explicitly require only passive obedience." And this is true, he admits. In an undemocratic era, taking an active part in politics was not only impossible for ordinary people; it would often have been construed as rebellious. But he continues,

. . . when action can be effective for good, a passive policy can only be justified by appeal to the concept of the whole of society being outside God's active care and providence. If what we have said about God's concern and providential care for society (i.e. control day by day) is true, then a merely passive role is unthinkable in a democracy where laws are moulded by citizens.
. . . To fail to get involved is to opt out of our God-given responsibilities as citizens.[29]

According to Stephen Monsma, "If man were perfect, politics would not be necessary: if man were totally without goodness, politics would not be possible."[30] But politics is both possible and necessary because of the nature of man.

Monsma, who has been chairman of the political science department at Calvin College in Grand Rapids, Michigan, and who recently ran for office in the U. S. House of Representatives, has suggested a number of criteria for making political decisions. "The purpose of politics," he posits, "is to establish an order which maximizes man's true freedom, that is, man's opportunity to develop and exercise his creative capacities in keeping with God's law of love."[31] He continues,

> To achieve this true freedom, society must engage in a balancing process, weighing the expansion of freedom resulting from safeguarding a certain right against the contraction of freedom resulting from the imposition of the obligations necessitated by the safeguarding of that right.
>
> [This] does not lead to government's seeking to force everyone to live creative, loving lives. The emphasis is on freedom, not on futile attempts to force persons to be creative and loving. . . .[32]

On the other hand,

> . . . the tragic history of workers exploited by employers, racial minorities suppressed by majority groups, consumers bilked by unscrupulous businessmen, gives testimony to where man's excessive self-love leads when government's regulative role is weak or missing. . . . Therefore, acts of persons which would be destructive of others' opportunities to act creatively in love must be thwarted by government action, but the goal and criterion is freedom.[33]

In making political choices, Monsma asks several questions:

1. Is the social or economic ill resulting in a loss of freedom for a segment of society?
2. Would the proposed political solution to the freedom-reducing ill result in a net gain of freedom for society?
3. What is the relative number of persons who would gain rights or advantages and obligations or disadvantages?
4. What is the relative importance and value of the rights or obligations, advantages or disadvantages, being imposed?
5. Is there any other alternative available (either political or nonpolitical) which would result in a larger net gain of true freedom for society?[34]

At the international level, Monsma continues to apply these criteria. Here, Monsma suggests, America's primary responsibility is to safeguard the freedom, including the economic freedom, of her own citizens. But America also has a duty to act justly toward other nations:

> The prime responsibility of foreign policy-makers toward the citizens of their own country is one half of a dual responsibility. The other half is to act toward other countries with justice . . . so to act toward them that they are not hindered in fulfilling the purpose they ought to be fulfilling for their citizens. This purpose, in turn, is to protect and maximize the true freedom of their citizens. . . . Each government, therefore, has an obligation to so conduct its foreign policy that it does not hinder other governments in the performance of their purpose. . . .[35]

Monsma develops this point specifically:

> In the area of trade policies, for example, the decision-maker has a responsibility to protect economic opportunities and stability within his country, but he also has a responsibility not to use the economic power of his country to plunder and wreck the economy of some other nation. . . .
>
> Such goals as I am proposing here would condemn the trade policies the United States and most of the industrialized countries follow toward the poor, largely agricultural, countries, policies which erect barriers against the importation of goods produced by these countries and result in millions in these countries being jobless. The rich countries, including the United States, obviously have a responsibility to their own people which includes protecting them from economic disadvantages and hardships. But when a super-rich country such as the United States follows trade policies which make it virtually impossible for other nations and their governments to develop strong, viable economies which can provide their citizens with the steady employment and decent wages necessary for a full, creative life, the United States is in the wrong.[36]

American citizens can affect private and public international policies. This is part of community development in poor countries, as much as sending a missionary doctor or the money to dig a well. In the well-researched *The Politics of Altruism,* Jorgen Lissner shows that Christian relief and development agencies tend to sidestep the former approach because it is potentially divisive.

Or they advocate one strategy to one audience and a different strategy to another audience.

An agency may well argue,

> We would immediately antagonize and alienate a significant part of our constituency if we came out asserting that the First World enriches itself at the expense of the Third World. Many people would simply stop supporting us financially. What is the use of having morally clean but financially empty hands? The important thing is to raise funds, so that we can support worthwhile activities in the Third World: others who do not risk being put out of business will have to tell the unpleasant truth.[37]

Yet such a set of priorities leaves a sour taste in the mouths of the poor who feel they are victims of repressive power plays originating in the West. Some relief and development organizations have owned up to this. Oxfam-Canada has said in print:

> We can no longer appear to be solely pre-occupied in the intricate and demanding business of raising and dispersing funds while we know that fundamental social, economic and political injustices exist which all of the aid in the world will never remove. We are at a point in our history when we run the risk of being seen as lacking in conviction and honesty if we do not show that we understand the underlying causes of poverty and underdevelopment, that we are unwilling to tolerate them, and that we wish to remove them insofar as we can. . . .[38]

The Mennonite Central Committee also has gone on record, in their statement of goals, for political solidarity as well as medical, agricultural, business, and relief solidarity. Their objectives are as follows:

> "To share resources in the name of Christ and proclaim Jesus as Lord; to establish and preserve an identity as free as possible from those nationalistic, cultural and ideological interests which are contrary to our understanding of faithfulness to Christ, and to seek to meet human need in any nation regardless of political identity or affiliation; to participate in a development process based on local capacity and self-reliance, by which persons and societies come to realize the full potential of their human, natural and spiritual resources; to follow the example of Christ in striving for justice, in identifying with the weak and oppressed and in reconciling the oppressor and oppressed; to provide

relief for victims of disasters in ways which encourage their maximum initiative, dignity and participation."[39]

Does your mission or favorite development agency have the courage to tackle the root causes of poverty? Prod them to do so. Support them when they do.

Reforms, of course, can never deal with basic moral issues, because these are a matter of personal attitudes. Such attitudes can be changed only when we humbly accept God's forgiveness and regeneration. Redemption is not an infection of social structures, though restored individuals may generate shock waves of reform. Material progress does not bring moral progress. Christ knew this, so he came into the world to save sinners—not to enable us to go on sinning in material comfort.

Besides, there are plenty of liberals and humanists and philanthropic Jews and even Arabs who have rolled up their sleeves to battle poverty. Amid this struggle, we dare not neglect what we alone can give. As A. N. Triton says, "We must treat the symptoms of evil, but when no one else knows how to get at the disease itself we would be totally irresponsible if we abandoned what we alone can do and became wholly occupied with the palliative."[40]

On the other hand, we are not only evangelists. We are also consumers who consider it our right to complain about cars that are lemons and other shoddy products. Many of us are parents who attend PTA meetings and voice our opinions. We are TV viewers, and some of us have campaigned against violence and immorality on the screen. We enjoy sports—playing handball, swimming, backpacking, jogging, or just watching Monday-night football. We relish food and music. God has created us to be multifaceted people, not just evangelists. He intends for us to enjoy his world. He also commissions us to battle for his dominion, his reign, over his own property and people (Gen. 1:28).

William Wilberforce was one of the English dandies of the frivolous eighteenth century. As a pampered boy from a wealthy family he joked, sang, preened—and worked very little. At Cambridge, where he had plenty of money to squander, "'books meant less than friends idling their time away, fortified by a great Yorkshire pie.'" Years later he wrote of his relatives and tutors, "'I'm sure that as much pains were taken to make me idle as were ever taken to make anyone else studious.'"[41]

Wilberforce had a number of limitations. He married unwisely. Like many of his age, he was addicted to opium; he took twelve grains daily for about thirty years. He was an erratic correspondent: "Alps upon alps!" he would moan as he looked at the piles of correspondence he had put off answering—and then he would answer the same letter for three days in a row.

In spite of his limitations, after his evangelical conversion, Wilberforce developed a new accountability. He conferred with the ex-slave trader John Newton: Given the compromise of politics, should he continue in Parliament? Newton encouraged him: "It is hoped and believed that the Lord has raised you up for the good of his church and for the good of the nation."

History suggests that Newton was right. Wilberforce set up programs for prison reform, medical aid for the poor, schools for the poor, child labor laws, clergy training, advocacy for convicts, and resettlement of freed slaves in Liberia.

Later critics have accused Wilberforce, whether justifiably or not, of being a moral busybody because of his campaigns to "make goodness fashionable." They have also charged that he did not empathize with the poor, since for complex reasons he voted conservatively on the corn laws, habaeus corpus, and various liberties which carried the scent of the French Revolution.

Whatever the criticisms of him, Wilberforce was a well-intentioned and generous man. He was one of the founders of the "Bettering Society," which developed into the Royal Institute. He gave away much of his wealth to personal charity cases. Even when he was blackmailed, he tactfully took the initiative to find a job for the widow of his blackmailer. Wilberforce also wrote a 491-page book, *A Practical View of the Prevailing Religious System of Professed Christians, in the Higher and Middle Classes of This Country, Contrasted with Real Christianity*. This became a classic in many homes. Throughout his administration, William Pitt looked to Wilberforce for moral advice.

What Wilberforce is remembered for most, however, is his lobbying—courageously, pragmatically, and humbly—for the abolition of the slave trade. In some of his speeches he resembles Daniel or Moses taking on their own shoulders the sins of Israel: "'I mean not to accuse anyone but to take the shame upon myself, in common indeed with the whole Parliament of Great Britain, for having suffered this horrid trade to be carried on under their authority. We are all guilty—we ought all to plead guilty, and not to exculpate ourselves by throwing the blame on others.'"[42]

After twenty years of sustained work, Wilberforce succeeded: English participation in the slave trade was prohibited. A natural outgrowth of this prohibition soon followed, according to historian Earl Cairns:

> Evangelical public opinion, working through the English delegate to the Congress of Vienna in 1815, was able to bring about the outlawing of the slave trade by most European states. This was at great cost to the English taxpayer because Spain and Portugal gave their consent only when they were promised P.10,500,000.00 from the English treasury. Slavery was ended in all British possessions by an act passed in 1833. The act provided nearly P.650,000,000.00 to compensate the owners who freed 700,000 slaves. These achievements would have been impossible without the work of Wilberforce and his evangelical friends in Parliament.[43]

From a Christian perspective, is politics significant?
What would be the opinion of the freed slaves?
Politics matters.

Thus the Bangladesh Rural Advancement Committee dares to come into conflict with local leaders and landowners in Bangladesh. Thus Brazilian fishermen dare to create new structures that bypass middlemen. Thus Lee Kwan Yew, with firm control of the conditions, solicits transnational businesses, while Anthony Campolo and the Interfaith Center for Corporate Responsibility confront them. Thus Juan Perez Alfonzo of Venezuela laments that development requires more than money; it requires better social and economic structures.

During the thick of his struggle, Wilberforce once wrote to a friend, "'If I thought the immediate Abolition of the Slave Trade would cause an insurrection in our [West Indian] islands [and therefore serious economic disruption], I should not for an instant remit my most strenuous endeavours.'"[44]

Do we dare to be that ethical about our national and international earnings?

1. Frances Moore Lappe and Joseph Collins, *World Hunger: Ten Myths* (San Francisco: Institute for Food and Development Policy, 1980), p. 8.

2. Arthur Beals, "Dear Mr. Harvey . . . : An Open Letter to Paul Harvey," *World Concern Update*, Feb. 1980, p. 6.

3. Ronald Sider, *Christ and Violence* (Scottdale, Pa.: Herald Press, 1979), p. 74.

4. Beals, "Dear Mr. Harvey," p. 6.

5. José Miguez Bonino, "Christians and the Political Revolution," in *The Development Apocalypse* (Geneva, Switzerland: World Council of Churches, 1967), pp. 103-104.

6. Frances Moore Lappe, Joseph Collins, and David Kinley, *Aid as Obstacle: Twenty Questions about our Foreign Aid and the Hungry* (San Francisco: Institute for Food and Development Policy, 1980), p. 72.

7. *Ibid.,* pp. 75-76.

8. Juan Perez Alfonzo, quoted in *Oregon Statesman*, Oct. 10, 1978.

9. Lappe, Collins, and Kinley, *Aid as Obstacle*, pp. 143-146.

10. Penny Lernoux, *Cry of the People* (Garden City, N.Y.: Doubleday, 1980), pp. 395-398.

11. Lappe, Collins, and Kinley, *Aid as Obstacle*, pp. 139-140.

12. In contrast to this, at the Philippines Missionary Conference in 1971, missionary Dick Dowsett argued, "Missionaries normally keep quiet, concentrating on a pietistic type of salvation, quietening their conscience by saying, 'We are guests here, we have no business to criticize.' But when we behave like this we are *not* neutral, we are simply supporting the status quo. That is often a terrible thing to do, for Christianity is not the same as middle-class conservatism. Oh for a return of the spirit of prophecy to our ministries. Amos was told to go home to Judah or shut up. But he did not use the 'guest' excuse." (Quoted in Michael Griffiths' *The Church and World Mission* [Grand Rapids, Mich.: Zondervan Publishing House, 1980], p. 101.)

13. John Sommer, *Beyond Charity: U.S. Voluntary Aid for a Changing Third World* (Washington, D.C.: Overseas Development Council, 1977), p. 7.

14. David Beckmann, *Where Faith and Economics Meet: A Christian Critique* (Minneapolis, Minn.: Augsburg Publishing House, 1981), p. 99.

15. "Into the Ranks of the Rich," cover story, *Time* (Asian edition), January 25, 1982, pp. 4-13; "Singapore: Searching for a Soul," cover story, *Far Eastern Economic Review*, May 7, 1982.

16. George Fuller, "Making Business Behave," *Eternity*, May 1980, p. 17.

17. For a discussion of this, see Mary Evelyn Jegen and Charles Wilber, *Growth with Equity* (New York: Paulist Press, 1979); Richard Barnet and Ronald Muller, *Global Reach: The Power of the Multinational Corporations* (New York: Simon & Schuster, 1975); and Lernoux, *Cry of the People*.

18. Gustavo Gutierrez, *A Theology of Liberation* (Maryknoll, N.Y.: Orbis Books, 1973), p. 26.

19. Fuller, "Making Business Behave," p. 19.

20. *Ibid.*

21. Anthony Campolo, "The Greening of Gulf and Western," *Eternity,* Jan. 1981, pp. 30-32.

22. *Ibid.*

23. *Ibid.*

24. *Ibid.*

25. Fuller, "Making Business Behave," p. 20.

26. *Ibid.,* pp. 20-21.

27. *Ibid.,* p. 22.

28. The addresses of these organizations are as follows: Interfaith Center for Corporate Responsibility, #566, 475 Riverside Drive, New York, NY 10027; and Bread for the World, 32 Union Square East, New York, NY 10003.

29. A. N. Triton, *Whose World?* (Leicester, England: Inter-Varsity Press, Universities and Colleges Christian Fellowship, 1970), p. 55.

30. Stephen Monsma, *The Unraveling of America* (Downers Grove, Ill.: Inter-Varsity Press, 1974), p. 40.

31. *Ibid.,* p. 62.

32. *Ibid.,* p. 53.

33. *Ibid.,* p. 65.

34. *Ibid.,* p. 64.

35. *Ibid.,* p. 123.

36. *Ibid.,* pp. 200-202.

37. Jorgen Lissner, *The Politics of Altruism: A Study of the Political Behavior of Voluntary Development Agencies* (Geneva, Switzerland: Lutheran World Federation Department of Studies, 1977), p. 187.

38. Oxfam-Canada, "Education," *Development Assistance Committee Review,* OECD, 1973-1974, pp. 1-3.

39. The Mennonite Central Committee, quoted in Sommer, *Beyond Charity,* p. 40.

40. Triton, *Whose World?* p. 68.

41. William Wilberforce, quoted in John Pollock's *Wilberforce* (London: Lion Publishing, 1977), pp. 8, 9.

42. *Ibid.,* p. 38.

43. Earl E. Cairns, *Christianity Through the Centuries* (Grand Rapids, Mich.: Zondervan Publishing House, 1954), p. 432.

44. Wilberforce, quoted in Pollock's *Wilberforce,* p. 89.

CHAPTER 5

REFUGEES
Helping People Take Root

 F OUR towering philodendron plants are marched to the front to flank a pulpit, transforming the gym into a church. Teenagers and grandparents wrestle folding chairs into gently curving rows. A baby—a "real American," I am told—sits spraddle-legged in the aisle, sucking a bottle. The Vietnamese church in Long Beach rises to sing its morning hymn. "We're marching to Zion, that beautiful city of God."[1]

For the time being, however, Thi has traded the cool greenery of the city of Dalat for the smog of the city of Los Angeles. Ong has left the smells of Saigon, of *nuoc mam* fish sauce and frangipani blossoms, for the smells of exhaust fumes. All the same, this morning they have inched along freeways to get here, to glimpse together the city they have not yet reached. Half of these hundred people have become Christians since leaving Vietnam.

Refugees. People uprooted. From 1900 to World War II, there were an estimated thirty million refugees, defined by the United Nations as people who crossed national boundaries because of their relation to their government. (The U.S. definition excludes peoples who have engaged in persecution.) During World War II, there were forty million refugees. Since then there have been seventy million. Today twelve million refugees camp around the world.[2] The great majority have no interest in or chance of coming to the United States. Tibetans have settled in India. Argentinians spice many Latin American nations. Afghans pitch their tents in Pakistan. Ethiopian Somalis have poured into desert Somalia, where they live in thirty-five camps. Christians minister to these uprooted people by providing rehabilitation. Just as Indians shared supplies with and taught skills to our uprooted pilgrim forefathers, so Christians help in refugee communities today.

Take Somalia, the fourth-poorest nation in the world. Refugees have increased Somalia's population by one-fifth—the equivalent

of sixty million people invading the United States. Here, according
to World Concern director Art Beals,

> If you were to remove the technical inputs, the food and mate-
> rial resources, the human resources of doctors, nurses, agrono-
> mists, water specialists, construction engineers, community
> development workers, supply officers and mechanics, the frag-
> ile fabric that holds this land together would fall apart. It would
> not only assign 1½ million refugees to probable death by dis-
> ease and starvation but . . . it would probably sound the death
> knell of the whole country.[3]

But because Christians and others have reached out, Somalia's
refugees no longer starve.

Some refugees need to be resettled. The United States accepts
twice as many foreigners as all the rest of the world's nations
combined.[4] Yet, according to an article by Leonard Reed, "in terms
of the number of Indochinese refugees resettled in proportion to
host country population, the United States is just slightly ahead of
Norway, Belgium, and New Zealand—but does less than half as
much as France and only one quarter as much as Australia."[5]

If present trends continue, immigration will add thirty-five million people to the U. S. population by the year 2000. Yet many
believe along with Colorado's governor Richard Lamm, "'The
economic pie is not growing and the day of the frontier is over. . . .
America cannot become the lifeboat of all the excess population
floating around.'"[6] A 1980 Roper poll found that eighty percent of
the interviewees wanted to reduce the number of immigrants
coming to the United States. "What about our own poor?" many
Americans protest. "Should we just forget about them, focusing
most of our attention on needy foreigners?"

A refugee in Oregon has fourteen children. Today she and three
of her daughters are enrolled at Williamette University, a good
private school. Next year this middle-aged mother will enjoy living
in Paris as an exchange student.

"How does she get this opportunity?" asks a thoughtful local
farmer. "My kids would like to go to France, too. They'll be lucky
just to afford college. At a state school. And I have four children—
not fourteen."

Blacks in New Orleans, Chicanos in Denver, and Metis in
Canada have protested what they see as an inordinate channeling

of funds and aid programs to the Indochinese when these older minorities need better housing, schooling, job opportunities, health care, and legal aid, and fair police protection.

"How many Americans will huddle in freezing flats this winter? How many look on from shacks in Appalachia or from rat-infested slums of the central cities? Our policy should be the same as Japan's: Aid, yes, immigration, no," says a Californian.

Perhaps, however, it is not so much our belated concern for the Indochinese as our lack of concern for other groups that is disproportionate. God's people were strangers in Egypt. Because of that, he required them to love strangers as well as the poor.[7]

Earlier this year, a middle-aged man hopped from one foot to the other in excitement, waiting at the airport for the refugees he was helping. Himself a "displaced person" from Europe in World War II, he could hardly wait to repay the hospitality that had been shown him. Spiritually, we as Gentiles have all been displaced persons, "strangers from the covenant of promise" (Eph. 2:12). Historically, too, our ancestors were strangers in America. "Love ye therefore the stranger: for ye were strangers. . ." (Deut. 10:19). Following this command is often rewarding: being hospitable to strangers may turn out to be as enriching an experience as if we'd been entertaining angels (Heb. 13:2).

So what can we do? At the pragmatic level, we can employ a refugee as a weekly or monthly housecleaner, a gardener, or a babysitter. Or, better still, place him in a full-time job. We can help a refugee practice English conversation. We can exchange visits. A refugee church or agency can offer you a myriad of opportunities to help.

Suppose you want to visit people who don't speak much English. Here are some tips:

- Take a *3x5 card* listing your name, address, and phone number.
- Take a small *gift*, like fruit or flowers.
- Take a small family *photo album*, including pictures of your parents, grandparents, brothers and sisters, children, nieces and nephews, and places where you have lived. This may inspire them to share photos of their family.
- If you enjoy a *craft* which is easily transportable, like embroidery or carving, take this along. It will help to make the

atmosphere more informal, give you something specific to talk about, and may encourage them to bring out some project that they are working on.

- Take *paper and pens,* so that you and they can draw pictures of what you lack words for.
- A *map* of the world may be familiar to them. If so, they can trace for you the routes of their journeys, point out where their various friends and relatives are currently living, etc. You too may trace the migrations of your ancestors, and your own moves from place to place.
- A *Sears catalog* often draws shy housewives into conversation.
- Take *nonverbal games,* which include puzzles, dominoes, chess, etc.
- *How-to books,* written on practical subjects like baby care or car mechanics and illustrated with lots of diagrams and photos, may spark interest.
- A *cassette* of music, a musical *instrument, slides,* or home *movies* are other possibilities for sparking interest and conversation.
- Handicraft material for the *children* of the family—even simple Play Doh—may provide entertainment for all.
- You may take turns learning bits of each other's *language*— the numbers from one to ten, names for common objects, etc. Putting yourself in a learning situation similar to theirs may expand your empathy as well as their entertainment.

Suppose you want to "sponsor" a refugee, perhaps an Indochinese refugee. What's involved?

Your group applies to an agency like the World Relief Refugee Service (P. O. Box WRC, Nyack, N. Y. 10960). You tell them what size family you can support. They'll consult with you. When you know who is coming, gather appropriate clothes and household goods and find a temporary place for them to live.

Meet them at the airport. You may feel more secure if you invite a bilingual Indochinese to come over and interpret for you the first evening you spend with your family. Or your whole group may rediscover what fun pantomiming is. A couple of days later, register them at a Social Security office and with the nearest public health office. Present them with I. D. bracelets with their address inscribed on them. If necessary, gradually introduce them to the "necessities" of American life: stoves, toilets, running water, telephones, public transportation, credit cards, et cetera. In some states, driver's license exams may be taken in an Indochinese language.

Let them eat rice, even three times a day. Provide meat, vegetables, and fruit. Flavor dishes with garlic, pepper, or curry. After you acquaint them with the stove, invite them to cook; you may learn some new techniques. Avoid dairy products and fast foods.

Enroll the children in school. Many districts have or will hire Indochinese communication assistants. Go with the adults to a job counseling center; ask your sponsoring agency or the Department of Social and Health Services in your state to direct you. They may be able to find jobs in which speaking English isn't that important; many employers are eager to use non-English-speaking laborers as seamstresses or construction workers, for example. Regardless of the employment possibilities, enroll the adults in a course that teaches English as a second language. If no such course is offered in the community colleges around you, maybe your church will set up regular opportunities for the family to engage in English conversation. Mine has.

You are not legally responsible for the family in any way. You may enroll them in programs in which they are eligible to receive food stamps, Medicare, and even welfare for eighteen months. (Of the 200,000 Indochinese who flooded the United States in 1975, ninety-five percent of those who are employable are now self-supporting. No other refugee group has such a high record.)

"But would I have the emotional and physical strength to carry through?" you may ask. Check to see what you devote your time to now. Shopping. Lunches. Committees. Redecorating your house. Doing macrame. Watching football. Growing plants. Trying recipes. Dwelling on your own problems.

You—if you share the responsibility with a dozen others—have time to befriend a refugee. After all, you too are supposed to be traveling light as a pilgrim.

Beyond the pragmatic and logistical level is the cultural level. We neglect it at our peril. Twelve million homeless people worldwide need short-term charity before they need long-term development. Yet, though they are in need, they are not merely needy. They remain human beings as complex and as common as we are. What do we need to know about the culture of displaced people from another part of the world? As an example, let's look at

Vietnamese culture. The issues raised will suggest questions relevant for many peoples.

To relate to Vietnamese effectively, we need to understand their ideas about the family, communication, optimism, and ambition.

• *Family.* Vietnamese have stronger families than Americans do. Older people are treasured in a way that we, in our preoccupation with youth, find hard to fathom. We print pictures of needy children to solicit aid. But if the refugees were in our place, they might well publish pictures of our elderly. "After all," they say, "we can always make children. But our elders are irreplaceable."

At the same time, they include more relatives in the "family" than we do.

"Who's that man in relation to you?" a refugee may be asked during an interview.

"He's my brother."

"Wait a minute. Isn't he your father's brother's son?"

"Yes. He's my brother."

Imagine the ache, then, when Hung has cousins in an Indonesian camp, and more cousins in a Malaysian camp. His father is still in Vietnam, and his mother, a Christian, has just escaped to China. A sister has managed to slip away to Hong Kong.

So each time you visit, ask, "How is your mother? Your cousin? Your nephew?" The sponsor who listens, instead of switching immediately to talk about bargains or car mechanics or recipes, will be loved.

In the family, Vietnamese parents expect obedience. Parents "have experience," they "see further than their children," I was told time and again. Unmarried adults live with their parents and, in many cases, turn over their salary to their mother, receiving only an allowance.

"How else do you think so many of us could own our own homes just four years after arriving here?" asks one mother.

"Living at home doesn't cost much, and it gives enjoyment to the parents," a pastor explains. "If their children follow the American customs too quickly, the parents feel that something is lost. The children learn, but they learn too much. American parents give their children too much freedom. And the children don't know how to handle it. They have no fence to keep them from temptation."

"To say you're a Christian, and your children don't respect

you—it's a contradiction," says one Vietnamese businesswoman. Sponsors, beware.

On the positive side, encourage family parties. Candles, flowers, incense, banners, pets (birds and fish), and nuances of language in poetry, proverbs, and metaphors—all will add to their delight.

• *Communication.* Vietnamese appreciate subtlety. Repartee that is rough or sarcastic may wound them. An exchange between an American sponsor painting a fence with his Vietnamese friend illustrates the point. During their small talk, the young Vietnamese asked, "What made you decide to sponsor *me?*

"Oh, I don't know what possessed me to make such a stupid choice," joked the sponsor.

It took a lot of mediation to assuage the refugee's hurt.

For young children in Vietnam, weaning, toilet training, and table manners were treated casually, but learning to greet people politely and correctly was drilled into them. But in America they find that informality is the style. Soon a girl wants to date like her classmates do. A boy wants an allowance. Because children become acculturated faster than adults, they have to interpret for their parents. The parents feel dependent or confused. All they know is the past; they don't know what's right and wrong in this society. They don't know how to provide legitimate authority.

How can a sponsor mediate such generation gaps? Jerrold Schecter describes the alternatives in *The New Face of Buddha:*

> There are three ways to deal with the Vietnamese. One is the French way, which says "Do this!" The second is the American way, which says, "This is the way we do things back home." And the third is the Vietnamese way: you just don't say anything, but you are patient and you wait, and you show by your actions that you respect the Vietnamese and are willing to listen to him. You don't ask him to tell you personal things, but you wait until he asks your advice.[8]

By implication and analogy more than by assertion, a sponsor must acquaint the refugees with alternatives that they may not be aware of. Give examples: "I had another friend who was in a situation like this, and she finally decided to. . . ." Then listen to see if they want to hear any more.

• *Optimism.* If American frankness jars Vietnamese, so does American optimism. There is a steady increase in psychological problems among Vietnamese who came to the United States in 1975, even though they're holding down good jobs, buying houses, and learning English. At first they suffered from anxiety. Now it's settled into depression.

"You sit here and you've got more things than you ever dreamed of. But your mother is in Vietnam. And all you know is that six months ago she didn't have enough rice," one explains.

In a Buddhist version of the Gospel written by a Thai, a blind beggar named Simon went to the market every day. Vendors greeted him companionably. Birds sang. Children laughed. A girl named Ruth befriended him, and they fell in love.

When Jesus touched those blind eyes, Simon's tranquil routine was shattered. Suddenly he saw the rags, the cheating, the sewage, and the gross burn that oozed where Ruth's face should have been. Sickened, he drew back from her.

Simon's horror culminated when he watched the crucifixion. He fell to his knees and cried, "God, give me back my blindness!"

This is a Buddhist response to the Gospel.[9]

The tumultuous history of the Vietnamese has taught them to identify with the enigmatic, smiling silence of the seated Buddha. "Only silence and music can express the inexpressible," Aldous Huxley once said. Refugees do not need us to smother them with superficial optimism; they need us to sit in silence with them, to weep with those who weep, to empathize with their sadness and loss. Perhaps it would be a good idea to write to the U. S. government or to the U.N. about some of their relatives. However useless the gesture (and it may not be), it may provide comfort. We must also remember that Vietnamese Christians have a history of faith marked by the sacrifice of martyrs during regular waves of persecution—in the 1830's, the 1850's, the 1880's, right up to the present. They need humble sharing, not cheap cheerfulness.

We Americans have believed that progress, not frustration, is the last word. Any problem can be solved if we put enough effort into it. We're practical, not contemplative. We measure everything: time, personality, even adjustment in relationships. And we put "Smile" bumper stickers on our cars.

Yet foreigners find us amazingly ignorant about the rest of the world, and correlate our optimism with our naiveté. While others suffer, we pamper our pets in ways that amaze people from other cultures. One Vietnamese has wryly remarked, "In my next life, I'd like to come back as an American dog!"

Even Christians, once each of us finds "God's will for *my* life," are complacent—instead of eager to reinvest all our energies in God's will for the world.

Empathy doesn't mean inaction. The Bible pulsates with passions. "God *so loved* the world. . . ." "The love of Christ *constrains* us. . . ." "We *press* toward the mark. . . ." Unlike the Buddhists, we don't repress our desires. Instead, we channel them toward the only adequate object. This in turn moves us to get involved with needy people like the refugees.

But not glibly. When I learned that a friend's much-loved mother had starved to death in Vietnam last week, I marched into my toddler's room and hurled his "It's Fun to Be a Christian" Frisbee into the garbage. For my friend's mother, being a Christian was far more than fun.

Differences in family patterns, communication styles, levels of optimism—all can be blocks to successful communication with refugees. So can misunderstanding their ambitions. Vietnamese are not overly optimistic, but they are ambitious. They are proud of 4,000 years of glorious history. At first they may work at any job. But a technician is not a farmer. Eventually he will switch to a position that uses his unique gifts.

Some Vietnamese will forego food for the status of a color TV. For others, status is education—and college is not enough.

"With your halting English, how can you expect to go so far?" the perplexed sponsor asks.

"Others came here without a single English word in their mouths, and they went to Harvard and Princeton. Why can't we?" a Vietnamese retorts.

But in some cases they are unrealistically comparing their prospects with those of the better-educated refugees who migrated here in 1975.

In general, Vietnamese immigrants have worked fervently. (That has become a problem: other Americans often look lazy by comparison. "Employers cannot get enough of them," said Robert Ray, Governor of Iowa, in 1979, after his state ᴜad accepted four thousand Vietnamese.)[10] Refugees from other countries, however, may have rather different work values. Carlos came from Ecuador to

New York City. Barbara Benjamin, a staff worker for Inter-Varsity Christian Fellowship, welcomed him. They were long-time friends. She was careful to get Carlos his first job with a Latin American employer, because the Latin would understand Carlos's casual attitude toward time and promptness.

Are U. S. work values essential? Time-consciousness, goal orientation, assertiveness, optimism, and frankness do increase productivity. Workers without these values are not desirable job risks. Yet how important is productivity? Many Latins ask us,

"Why are you so frank, when you could be courteous?"

"Why do you work like machines, instead of taking time to think for yourselves?"

Why do you live in the future instead of the present?"

"Why are your jobs more important than your families?"

These questions suggest the strengths of alternative values. Let's admit that productivity should be less pivotal than we Americans have allowed it to be. But then we can also show our refugee friends that certain American values lead to job retention, which leads to earning money, which leads to the fulfillment of certain material goals that they have.

At the same time, if we can find them work that uses the habits they developed and refined at home, so much the better. A small Presbyterian church in Seattle has helped sixteen Hmong and Minh Laotian families lease state land for farming. These tough hill farmers are right at home in the rain that falls so frequently there. In three months of harvest they have cleared $7,000 at farmers' markets. American volunteers help them with transportation, procurement of tools, bookkeeping, and marketing and legal advice.

Besides sharing work values, should we also share our faith? Again, let us consider the Vietnamese. At first, if a sponsor wants them to attend church, they probably will. If he presses them, "Will you believe in Jesus?" they may answer, "Oh, yes." But they cannot be bought. Our sponsorship does not give us the right to control their beliefs.

How can a sponsor communicate Christ to his Vietnamese friends?

"To show love is not enough. Many Americans have done that. You have to show faith, too," says one perceptive Vietnamese.

Do your refugees see you stop and pray in the middle of small crises? Do you explain to them how the Lord is providing for your emotional, social, and physical needs? Are you so filled with the presence of God that a certain love, holiness, and power walk through the door with you when you visit them? Traditionally, Vietnamese have assumed that the transcendent touched many details of their lives. By contrast, Americans look materialistic. Even Christian Americans.

Beyond this, introduce the refugees to Christian Vietnamese. From San Diego to Montreal are dozens of *Tin-Lanh* Vietnamese churches associated with the Christian and Missionary Alliance (the Alliance was the only Protestant mission in Vietnam until 1959), not to mention scores of others.

Ping-Pong at youth friendship centers. Camps. Conferences. "Prayer warrior" certificates. Helping new refugees, of whatever religion. The churches hum with activities and offerings. A complete range of Vietnamese Christian education curricula. *Thong Con* (Fellowship) magazine. A fledgling Vietnamese Bible school where on weekends college students absorb instruction about the Bible, theology, Christian ethics, church history, and Bible study methods; Vietnamese lectures complement English textbooks. Soccer, volleyball, basketball, decathlons, and tennis competitions—Vietnamese churches are filled with opportunities to learn and play.

Yet aren't ethnic churches segregated? Is there really no difference between Jew and Greek, between bond and free, between male and female, if Sunday at 11:00 A.M. remains the most segregated hour in America? Where is our unity? Where is our family-ness? Theologian Jurgen Moltmann argues that ethnic churches do not participate fully in the dynamics of Christian hope.[11] Christian statesman John Stott argues that heterogeneous congregations are stronger.[12]

Integration of the "huddled masses yearning to breathe free" has long been an American ideal. In 1914, the Ford Motor Company founded an English language institute for its immigrant employees. Graduation epitomized integration. A huge "Ford Melting Pot" glowed on stage at the ceremonies. Five hundred at a time, immigrants marched "into" the pot. They wore the garb of their homelands. The teachers stirred the pot with enormous ladles and—presto! Out popped the graduates, dressed in standard American clothes and waving American flags. Integration.[13]

Today, however, people are more determined to retain their

roots. During the 1960's we learned that Black was beautiful. Other ethnic groups are also rediscovering their own richness. The Christians among them put forward five reasons for ethnic churches:

1. God is glorified by diversity. God generated a world of amazing complexity and alternative models. He gifted man with the creativity that develops cultures. Christ affirmed foreigners (Matt. 25:33; Mark 7:26; Luke 7:2; John 4). God anticipates all peoples and tribes and kindreds and nations swirling around his throne in a kaleidoscope of color, not an undifferentiated beige mass.

One Christmas, a group from our Filipino church in Seattle went caroling up the steep, narrow stairs at an International District hotel, bringing holiday cheer to a bare lounge. Firm and brown and wrinkled as walnuts, old Filipinos sat around us. "Old-timers" who had lost their youth—and their opportunity for families—in the fish canneries and apple orchards of America in the days before it was legal to marry a white woman. Now, as they drummed their fingers softly in time to our music and gazed into space, what did they see?

Suddenly three young men glided in. Why were they here? Filipinos lived with their families. Only the lonely and homeless lived here. Were they Filipinos? Their eyes looked Chinese.

They listened. They looked at each other. One dashed out and returned with a book.

When we came to a break in our singing, they pressed together around the book and made signs that they wanted to sing for us.

> O happy day
> That fixed my choice
> On Thee, my Savior
> And my God. . . .

That was the tune. But the words were not from any Philippine language.

"They're Cambodians," whispered the hotelkeeper's wife.

Only recently had Christianity exploded in their country. In 1972, several thousand Cambodians responded to evangelistic campaigns. The number of churches in Phnom Penh jumped from two to twenty-seven. But by 1976, Cambodia was no more. The Khmer Republic had replaced it, waging a campaign of genocide comparable to the Jewish holocaust in World War II.

Yet here were these brothers in Christ singing "O Happy Day."
One verse. Three verses. Five. Eight.

Michael, my husband, managed to creak out some rusty French.
The young men smiled; communication at last! But their stories
were harrowing.

"Where is your family?"

"All dead. I'm alone."

"What about yours?"

"There is no word."

Here they were. They couldn't speak English. They couldn't
read the signs on the streets and the buses. They couldn't get a
driver's license. They couldn't go to school because they couldn't
understand the teachers. They didn't know how to find community services. Here they were, left alone among old men and harrowing memories to recreate their lives from the ground up.

Had I been in their shoes, would I have chosen to sing "O
Happy Day"? Yet it seems to be a Cambodian favorite. When the
Cambodian church that meets in my church recently baptized
eighteen people in popular Green Lake while joggers and skaters
whizzed by, what did their choir sing? "O Happy Day." Surely this
recent flowering of the Cambodian church is to God's glory. Surely
he wants them to preserve ethnic strengths that may complement
ours—such as the fresh understanding of what makes a day happy.

2. Every person has the right to worship God in his mother
tongue. There are many immigrants who want to worship in an
integrated group, and we must welcome them. There are many
others, however, who want to worship with familiar body pos-
tures, familiar music, familiar time schedules, familiar inclusion of
children and noise, and familiar church parties.

3. Ethnic churches have far more effective outreach in many
ethnic communities than do "melting pot" churches.

The Bible teaches centrifugal concern for the nations. It also
teaches centripetal concern, centering down, zeroing in on the
foreign visitors living among us. Take the first ten chapters of Acts.
Philip presents the Gospel to a foreign diplomat in Palestine.
Ananias takes it to an international student. Peter takes it to
Cornelius, a military man stationed overseas. Acts 2, the record of
the Pentecostal experience, demonstrates how the internationals
living in one city could be made excited about the Good News.[14]

Ethnic churches often can have excellent outreach to such

international visitors. In the Fellowship of Iranian Christians, for example, a fledgling group which burst onto the scene after the fall of the Shah and which is composed of semi-refugee Iranians in the United States, many of the new Christians do not even speak English. Worship services generally are in Farsi, the Iranian language.

4. Unless another cultural tradition is consciously made the basis for worship, the cultural tradition of the majority in the society will dominate, no matter how integrated the races of the members.

Circle Church in Chicago often has been held up as a model of integration. Yet within the past decade the Black members have left—because, they said they wanted to worship the funky Jesus rather than the honky Christ. Susan Okamoto, a third-generation Japanese American who speaks little Japanese, finds her church in Seattle distinguished from standard American churches by its communication, which is usually indirect: disagreements are expressed through passive resistance; expressions of humor are subtle; decision-making is a process in which everyone contributes a little to the deliberations; in evangelism, much attention is given to how a decision for Christ will affect the family; leadership is discreet and indirect; money planning is indirect ("a business meeting to discuss budgets would be offensive"); conflicts are settled indirectly.

Many Native American congregations have been contrasted with Anglo churches by the different emphases that characterize them:

Anglo Churches	*Native American Churches*
progress	harmony
mobility	ancestral land
dressing up	dressing simply
classical music, folk music	Indian music, country music
frank exchange of individual opinions	avoiding contradiction
much conversation	little conversation
conformity	privacy (members live far apart)
respecting youth and change	respecting elders and traditions
promptness	getting into the spirit, avoiding time boundaries

Members of integrated churches rarely have the anthropological sophistication to isolate these kinds of factors, and therefore to allow them to be significant in planning corporate life. So a *culturally* integrated church remains very rare. Do Moltmann or Stott know of any? It is far different from—and far more than—having a Black on the podium. In fact, an "ethnic" church *may* turn out to be as culturally integrated as any; it just adapts from a cultural base different from that of the majority. In a Hispanic church in New York, for example, Puerto Ricans, Cubans, South Americans, and Blacks work well together.

5. Ethnic churches can prepare foreign students and temporary workers to witness effectively when they return to their home countries. Those who return will not have to endure such radical culture shock. They will be able to identify the Christian faith not only with Americans but with their own people. And by preserving the culture the ethnic church may provide a kind of laboratory where they can experiment with creative worship, teaching, fellowship, and outreach patterns, drawing freely on the myriad resources available here in the United States.

In this age of jet travel, overseas visitors are not isolated from their home cultures. If we minister wisely to foreign visitors here, we can powerfully affect their family, friends, and colleagues at home. We do well always to think of them in that context.

Take Ethiopia, for example. Unusually malignant Marxist officials have been persecuting churches there. In country districts, Christians are electrocuted with crude wires. Can we help the Ethiopian church? In the United States is a fellowship of Ethiopian students, some of whom plan to return to provide Christian leadership. What we offer to the least of these, we offer to the church of Ethiopia.

Of course we must be united in Christ. Where there are ethnic churches, we can seek to establish joint projects. Cooperative worship services once a month. Joint committees for community-wide evangelism or benevolence projects. Sharing of equipment, like overhead projectors. Complementary sharing of services: for example, one church may run a day-care center; another may provide a college or Bible-school extension program; another may specialize in a marriage counseling service; another may have a resource for senior citizens. A Black church in North Carolina runs an extensive tutorial service, a college scholarship program, and a revolving "bank" that loans students college textbooks. They also provide a financial aid service which helps members get loans for homes and small businesses. A church in Chicago runs a legal aid clinic which serves people in a slum community, many of whom are arrested on false charges. A fellowship in Boston runs a "people bank," matching skilled volunteers with needs; Black, Anglo, and Spanish people participate. A church in Houston sponsors forty "extended families" who minister to delinquents, drug addicts, unmarried mothers, and mentally or physically handicapped people. A church in Seattle offers detailed financial counseling services for people who don't know how to get or keep jobs, or balance budgets.

We must be one family in Christ. Building truly needed bridges with ethnic churches can lay a foundation. If we don't, since American communities naturally are segmented along lines of race and social class, we may live all our lives without noticing people in other groups. And our lives will be incomplete.

In many cases, ethnic fellowships may form *within* our churches. South Main Baptist Church in Houston provides an example. In addition to an international women's club which has attracted over one hundred internationals, children's activities practically scheduled at the same time the club meets, and separate English classes for immigrant adults and teenagers, the church offers Sunday school classes for Chinese, Japanese, Koreans, and Hispanics. Interestingly, the Chinese, Koreans, and some of the Spanish members attend their classes as couples. But other Spanish members attend separate classes for men and women. The Japanese women have their own class, but the Japanese men prefer to attend a general integrated men's class. The Koreans have not only their own class but also their own worship services. South Main Baptist Church evidently is sensitive to the individual preferences of its ethnic groups.[15]

Giving is not a one-way street. Our world is overflowing with refugees who need food, shelter, medicine, and jobs. Our cities have hundreds of international students in English language institutes who beg for people to talk with them and to befriend them. Many of them will be world leaders in the 1990's. There is no need to spend five hundred dollars on a plane ticket to engage in cross-cultural missions. But we dare not dehumanize these needy people by giving without receiving. As they need our strengths, so we need theirs. In particular, in every region of the world today there is a Christian heritage that we need to learn from.

"Men of spiritual resources may not only redeem catastrophe, but turn it into a grand creative moment," wrote the Christian historian Herbert Butterfield. "The rarest creative achievements of the mind must come from great internal pressure, and are born of a high degree of distress. In other words, the world is not merely to be enjoyed but is an arena for moral striving. . . . History is in the business of making personalities"—conformed to the image of God.[16]

Can we learn from some of our refugee brothers and sisters how to "redeem catastrophe"?

When I attended a Vietnamese worship service in Long Beach, the Scripture reading was from Genesis 12: "Now the Lord had said unto Abram, 'Get thee out of thy country, and from thy kindred, and from thy father's house, unto a land that I will show thee: And I will make of thee a great nation and I will bless thee . . . and thou shalt be a blessing. . . .'"

Sandwiched between a grandmother dozing placidly, her hands folded over her stomach, and a shy young woman who had crossed the room to befriend in halting English this large white woman, now listening uncomprehendingly to the sermon being given in lilting Vietnamese, I turned to Hebrews for more about Abraham. I read about faith, the substance of things hoped for. And about people who died in faith—some receiving their dead raised to life again, and others tortured—not experiencing the fulfillment of their hopes, but persuaded of it, embracing it, confessing themselves strangers and pilgrims on earth.

In the Vietnamese church, I sat among people like this. People seeking a city still to come.

---

1. Parts of this chapter were first published in the article "From Refugees to Neighbors: How to Understand the Vietnamese Immigrants," *Eternity,* Dec. 1979, pp. 20-24.

2. World Refugee Survey, 1982, a publication of the U. S. Committee for Refugees.

3. Arthur Beals, "Dear Mr. Harvey . . . : An Open Letter to Paul Harvey," *World Concern Update,* Feb. 1980, p. 6.

4. "Closing the Golden Door," *Time,* May 18, 1981, p. 24.

5. Leonard Reed, "Legislation for a World in Tumult," *Saturday Review,* Sept. 15, 1979, p. 14.

6. Richard Lamm, quoted in "Closing the Golden Door," p. 26.

7. Many biblical passages deal with this command. Some refer to the Christian treatment of strangers (Lev. 19:33-34; Deut. 24:17ff.); others to the Christian response to the poor and needy (Deut. 26:12; Ps. 82:3-4; Isa. 1:17; 58:3-12; Zech. 7:10; Exod. 22:21; 23:9; Lev. 25:35; James 2:2-16; 1 John 3:17-19; Luke 14:12-13; Matt. 25:34-46).

8. Jerrold Schecter, *The New Face of Buddha* (New York: Coward-McCann, 1967), p. 152.

9. Kukrit Pramoj, "The Hell Which Heaven Forgot," *Practical Anthropology,* May-June 1966.

10. Robert Ray, quoted in "The Not-So-Promised Land?" *Time,* Sept. 10, 1979, p. 24.

11. Jurgen Moltmann, *Religion, Revolution, and the Future* (New York: Charles Scribner's Sons, 1969), p. 27.

12. John Stott, *Our Guilty Silence* (Grand Rapids, Mich.: Eerdmans, 1967), p. 71.

13. C. Peter Wagner, *Our Kind of People* (Atlanta: John Knox Press, 1979), p. 45.

14. Mark Hanna was the person who first brought this exegesis to my attention.

15. The ministry of South Main Baptist Church to internationals is described in Frank Obien's *Building Bridges of Love* (San Bernardino, Calif.: Campus Crusade for Christ, 1974), pp. 112-115.

16. Herbert Butterfield, *Christianity and History* (London: Fontana Books, 1957), pp. 101-102.

CHAPTER 6

THE KINGDOM OF GOD
A Treasury of Cultures

BLACK is not beautiful if you follow the ideas of William Shockley. Shockley is a Nobel Prize winner who shot into the news a few years ago when he pointed out that Blacks tend to score lower on I.Q. tests than Whites.

What to do about it? Sterilize the Blacks. Shockley proposed federally funded sterilization for those who got low scores. One analyst suggested that this could end up wiping out eighty-five percent of the Blacks in America—a nice clean civilized castration of a race.

What does an I.Q. test measure? Not everyone agreed that it measured intelligence adequately. Social scientists rose up to rebut Shockley and point out how our environment shapes the way we perform on tests.

And yet, if our environment determines us, we're still in prison. Theories of environmental determinism may be better than genetic theories of inferiority. But they still trap us in iron views of group differences. They still categorize human beings in ways that decrease options. They dampen creativity.

Mental models do matter. It is amazing what a little self-respect can do for a person. A good self-image is like a tank full of gas. There have been periods, for example, when I have left my bed unmade, justifying the chaos because I was chasing higher priorities. But not long ago a friend designed a batik quilt for me, one rippling with patches of blue, green, and brown. Now that bed gets smoothed out every morning. A vision of beauty spurs me to chisel a few minutes out of the morning bustle. In the same way, a graduate who receives a new Porsche polishes it like he never did the old Rambler. Mental models matter. Unfortunately, theories of environmental determinism limit and darken our positive visions of ourselves, and repress our growth.

Genetic determinism is one grid through which to view other races and cultures. Environmental determinism is another. Neither is an adequate perspective, but what is? Specifically, what is a Christian view? As we love our international neighbors through prayer, politics, and contributions, how should we evaluate their diverse heritages? Isn't there only one right way of life, if we follow the Bible? What is God's plan for different peoples—his "foreign policy"? How do different cultures fit into God's kingdom?

To form a Christian attitude toward cultures, we need to begin with our doctrine of man, our understanding of the nature of man. From a Christian perspective, although economic and political deprivation are real, people are never just "deprived elements." They are never just objects needing help. Even in the middle of squalor and violence there exist family affection and singing and children's games—and sometimes even dignity.

In other words, a person is more than his environment, or his heredity, or both. Don't we feel this about ourselves? We may be less than brilliant or even somewhat maladjusted, but we're not nothing. In fact, at times we feel infinitely valuable. What a little cosmos each of us is when we think the people and events around us matter only because we're interested in them. This is part of being a subject rather than an object.

Am I worth breeding—worth exempting from Shockley's hypothetical sterilization campaign? You have to answer this question for yourself. Do you base your value on hereditary endowment? Environmental adjustment? Or something else? As a Christian, I find myself valuable because God gave me a personality modeled after his own. I'm not just chemicals. I'm not just a machine. I'm a creator. So I can't be completely canned and served up in sociological statistics.

And yet, paradoxically, I am the enemy. Deprived by my environment, I selfishly deprive others by the environment I help create. Like an abused child, I abuse others. Optimistic humanists have assumed that man has within himself the power to develop a good society. Radical socialists and Marxists agree. But Christianity paints a strikingly different picture of the nature of man. Man is not the owner of the universe but a creature within it. Further, he is a creature who sins—who often willfully chooses what is false. He doesn't have within himself the power to live right continually.

In fact, of all these perspectives, the Christian view squares the best with our experience. And since World War II, optimistic humanism has been dying out as an intellectual force. When enlightened Germany seemed to go berserk and when the United States dropped the atomic bomb, many humanists began to despair of man's being able to build a good society.

Psychoanalysts Rollo May and Karl Menninger recently have reaffirmed the old belief that people are simultaneously both good and evil. In *Whatever Became of Sin?*, Menninger argues that we must rediscover and admit that we are sinners. He writes:

> Sin is the only hopeful view. The present world miasma and depression are partly the result of our self-induced conviction that since sin has ceased to be, only the neurotics need to be treated and the criminals punished. The rest may stand around and read the newspapers. Or look at television. Do your thing and keep your eye on the road leading to the main chance.
>
> As it is, vague, amorphous evil appears all about us, and when this or that awful thing is happening and this terrible thing goes on and that wretched circumstance has developed, and yet, withal, when no one is responsible, no one is guilty, no moral questions are asked, when there is, in short, nothing to do, we sink to despairing helplessness. . . .
>
> [But] if the concept of personal responsibility and answerability for ourselves and for others were to return to common acceptance, hope would return to the world with it.[1]

Among philosophers today, optimistic humanism is out-of-date. But many social activists of both the right and the left still cling to it implicitly. How else can they justify their continuing fascination with man and society? How else can they find motivation to keep going?

However, from a Christian point of view, in the words of Alexander Schmemann, a Russian orthodox priest,

> . . . this world is broken. Not absurd, not suspended between two vacuums, but something extremely precious and yet totally broken. The whole creation, which God proclaimed to be good, reflecting His glory, this world is broken. The more it is perfect, the more we can understand the tragedy, the tremendous sadness, of that brokenness. It is only when something precious is broken that we are sad. If something has no goodness in it, why cry about it? That something which is the image of the ineffable glory is wounded, bleeding, ugly: this is the

biblical intuition of evil. No, evil is not some mysterious "it." Evil is not the absence of good. Evil is the presence of brokenness, the free choice of man not to be in that wholeness and beauty.[2]

Precious and broken. Jesus told a story about that once. About a shepherd who had a statistically successful fold full of sheep: ninety-nine out of a hundred. But the abstract group wasn't what interested him. He was concerned about the single sheep that was missing. So he went out and searched for that one—and got more satisfaction from finding him than from seeing all the others docile in the fold. In his daily life, Jesus bore out that story. He spent a lot of time with physically, mentally, and socially oppressed people. And he offered all of them power in a personal relationship with God.

What is a Christian view of man, then? We are not just chemicals. We are not just machines. We're precious—and we're broken. So loving our neighbors will demand both hope and honesty. As we will see, we must respect their dignity in God's image. We must also safeguard ourselves against their depravity.

Our view of cultures takes root in this view of man. Again, a tension exists. On the one hand, cultures are marred by sin; on the other hand, they are a gift of God's common grace. Early in the Bible we discover God approving the physical world that he made, out of which people mold the material part of their cultures. God endowed people with creativity and commissioned them to rule and develop the world. And God gave people cultural structures within which to live and work.

God approved of the physical world. He delighted in the very soil that he gave his people. It was, in the words of Deuteronomy 8,

A good land, a land of brooks of water, of fountains and depths that spring out of valleys and hills;
A land of wheat, and barley, and vines, and fig trees, and pomegranates; a land of olive oil, and honey;
A land wherein thou shalt eat bread without scarceness, thou shalt not lack any thing in it; a land whose stones are iron, and out of whose hills thou mayest dig brass. (vv. 7-9)

God gave man oil to make his face shine, wine to make his heart glad, friends like iron to sharpen him, a wife like a fruitful vine, and children like arrows shot out of his bow. The marvel of a baby's body hints at how God—who could have made the world tasteless, scentless, and black-and-white—approves the physical world.

God endowed people with creativity, and commissioned them to rule and develop the world. What does it mean to be made in God's image? Theologians have suggested that it means that man is endowed with rationality, personality, moral sensitivity, love, freedom, dominion, and a capacity for relationships. Surely it also means that man is blessed with creativity. Creative symboling to any significant degree distinguishes man from animals. Creativity involves self-awareness, abstract thinking, the use of symbols, and freedom of choice. As God is a creator, we are made creative in his image. When we create, then, we are exercising a characteristic that particularly represents God.

Unleashing our creativity, we are to subdue the earth and have dominion over it. This is known as the "cultural mandate," which comes to us in the first chapter of Genesis. Erich Sauer says that God's words call us "to progressive growth in culture":

> Far from being something in conflict with God, cultural achievements are an essential attribute of the nobility of man as he possessed it in Paradise. Inventions and discoveries, the sciences and the arts, refinement and ennobling, in short, the advance of the human mind, are throughout the will of God. They are the taking possession of the earth by the royal human race, the performance of a commission. . . .[3]

A. A. Stockdale has commented,

> When God made the earth, he could have finished it. But he didn't. He left it as a raw material—to tease us, to tantalize us, to set us thinking, and experimenting, and risking, and adventuring. And therein we find our supreme interest in living.
> He gave us the challenge of raw materials, not the satisfaction of perfect, finished things.
> He left the music unsung, and the dramas unplayed.
> He left the poetry undreamed, in order that men and women might not become bored, but engaged in stimulating, exciting, creative activities that keep them thinking, working, experimenting, and experiencing all the joys and satisfactions of achievement.

God expects us to live and work heartily in subduing the earth. We are to have an abundant life. We are not merely to exist in quiet resignation but to press toward the goal ahead. We are to do everything heartily, as to the Lord. Whatever our hand finds to do, we are to do with all our might.

God not only approved the physical world and commissioned people to develop it. He also gave his blessing to cultural structures. In the beginning God said that it was not good for man to be alone; man was made to live in a community of meaning. So God gave man instructions about establishing the family, the state, work, worship, the arts, education—even festivals. For the Jews, for example, God spelled out laws which preserved a somewhat balanced ecology, ordered social relations, provided for sanitation, protected the rights of the weak, the blind, and the deaf, widows, orphans, and strangers, the poor and debtors—and gave duty a motivation by relating it to himself.

Culture is not something alien from God. Rather, it is in the words of H. R. Rookmaaker, "the result of man's creative activity within God-given structures."[4] All cultures may be seen as gifts of God's grace. Unfortunately, Victorian missionaries and Christian colonists, like others of their era, didn't often look at cultures that way. True, the pioneer missionary William Carey not only preached but also helped poor Indians start successful businesses. David Livingstone not only evangelized but also lobbied against the slave trade. Robert Morrison not only translated the Bible into Chinese but also set up vocational training schools. Yet much missionary "uplift" has been patronizing—a lifting-up to *our* standard of living, our family patterns, our forms of worship, even our pronunciations.

It was church-going Westerners who enslaved Africans, scattered poisoned meat around for Australian aborigines, enjoyed regular hunting seasons against Tasmanians, fought a war against China's pagan rulers in order to introduce opium into China, and broke innumerable promises to the American Indians. Ignorant Christian missionaries have condemned beautiful art, oral literature, and social regulations, as well as healthful food, housing, and working habits. Even today, Christianization often means Westernization. Faced with the world's rich cultural complexity, faced with the opportunity to be open-minded, to suspend judgment, to affirm people who are different, many missionaries instead tie everyone up in the same straitjacket. They do not see cultures as gifts of God's grace.

Certainly cultures with little Christian heritage may manifest God's blessings in unique ways. When I spent four years in the Philippines, for example, I discovered that my neighbors displayed God's goodness in a wealth of ways. They were a people with lithe, limber bodies. Skilled in the art of relaxation. Musically creative. Blessed with a heritage of economic freedom for women. They had enduring loyalties and strong families. Lavished a great deal of time on their children. Were warmly hospitable. Enjoyed being with a large number of people continuously. They took a real delight in sharing. Were able to live graciously on little money.

Since every good gift is from above and since all wisdom and knowledge come from Jesus Christ, these beautiful qualities of Philippine culture must be gifts of God. It seems that, just as our Creator delights in a vast variety of colors and smells, just as he has brought millions of unique personalities into being, so he has ordained an amazingly wide spectrum of cultures. He has programmed into man a capacity for cultural variation that enables us to explore our potential in all its complexity, to increase the richness of his world.

Culture is not neutral. Culture is God's gift. He has endowed people everywhere with his image, the image of a creator, with the creativity that develops cultures. He has commissioned us with the cultural mandate. Thus cultures are not a collection of amoral rules holding Hobbesian man in check; they are treasure chests of symbols that allow man to exuberantly express the image of God.

But there is, of course, another side to this: we and every aspect of our world and culture are spoiled by sin. Sin infests culture, plaguing us from cradle to grave. As Bob Dylan sings it,

> I was blinded by the devil,
> Born already ruined,
> Stone-cold, dead,
> As I stepped out of the womb.[5]

We ourselves once were dead in sin. But God has freed us, raised us to new life, and called us to fight against our old nature and old environment. So we are not to love the world or be conformed to it, but rather transformed by the renewing of our minds. We have received the Spirit of God in place of the spirit of the world. We are to set our affections on heaven above, not on the things of this earth. We have been crucified to the world. We are told that no man who wars entangles himself with the things of this life.

And the Bible applies this specifically to various areas of culture. Christian women are not to be caught up in the latest fashions but are to cultivate a meek and quiet spirit. In politics, we are not to agitate for some utopia but rather to nurture one another to prepare for life together in the kingdom of Christ. In intellectual pursuits, we are not to become absorbed in philosophy, because even a fool in Christ is wise. We are not to love money, not to worry about meeting expenses. We are not even to be slaves to schedules or productive work, as Martha was. We are not to worship aesthetic experiences; rather, we are to be like Abraham, willing to leave the centers of culture. Like Paul, who could stand on the Areopagus, looking out over one of the greatest artistic achievements of human culture, and shout that what is really worth knowing is Jesus Christ.

So we are caught in the tension between the good and the evil of culture. On the one hand, our culture—or any culture—is precious, a gift of God's common grace. On the other hand, every culture is a pattern of exploitation, due to our sinfulness. How do we handle this tension?

Although sin infects the entire world, God is still in charge. He still owns the cattle on a thousand hills. He still sends rain on the just and the unjust. He ordains governments, according to Romans 13. The structures of nature and society are held together in Christ, according to Colossians 1. God is moving in history toward his own goal. This is still his world. That was made irrevocably clear when God himself became human to reconcile the world to himself. He is now reconciling people to himself. Later he will deliver even nature from the bondage of corruption into the glorious liberty of the children of God, according to Romans 8. There will be a new heaven and a new earth. Even our flabby bodies will be glorified. And the kingdoms of this world will become the kingdom of our Lord.

God loves the world. Though he wants us to be crucified to a world-centered lifestyle, he does not want us to go out of the world. In fact, we can't go out. "The world" is not a set of institutions that we can condemn and avoid while we condone and support those that seem "set apart." No institution is pure. Whether we are in a tavern, on a tennis court, or even in a church board meeting, self-centeredness can be pervasive. And worldliness is, at bottom, attitudes which ignore God, self-centered or man-centered rather than God-centered or kingdom-centered.

We balance, then, between recognizing God's ownership in every area of culture and affirming it, and recognizing sin's potentiality and actuality in every area and judging it. If we do this, though we may get involved in many of the same activities that our non-Christian neighbors pursue—skiing, barbecuing, shopping, investing, clipping coupons—we will not get involved in our culture thoughtlessly. We are not to be conformists. But neither are we to be dropouts. Rather, we are to be creative deviants in the service of Christ and his kingdom.

The kingdom: that is what God calls his foreign policy, his plan for the diverse peoples in his multifaceted world.[6]

What was Jesus' basic message? Repent, for the kingdom of God is at hand.

What was his teaching? Unless you are born again, you cannot see the kingdom. Unless your righteousness exceeds that of the scribes and the Pharisees, you will not enter the kingdom. Blessed are the poor in spirit, for theirs is the kingdom.

His works served the kingdom: he cast out devils to show that the kingdom had come.

His parables were about the kingdom. The kingdom is like a mustard seed. The kingdom is like leaven. The kingdom is like a treasure hid in a field. The kingdom is like a net let down into the sea.

The core of his prayer was about the kingdom: "Thy kingdom come, thy will be done on earth as it is in heaven."

Right before he died, and again when he was about to ascend to heaven, he directed everyone's attention back to the kingdom.

The kingdom of God is a mystery. In one sense it exists in the future. When Christ reigns, there will be no need of the sun because the lamb-king will give off dazzling light. The wolf will lie down with the lamb, and the trees of the field will clap their hands. We will beat our swords into ploughshares, and every man will have a vine and a fig tree to invite his neighbor to sit under. Dromedaries from Muslim lands will come bearing rich gifts for Jesus. And the earth will be filled with the knowledge of God like water fills the sea.

In one sense the kingdom exists in the future. But in another
sense it is present, here and now. Jesus said, "If by the spirit of God
I cast out demons, then the kingdom of God has come upon you"
(Matt. 12:28); "Heal the sick . . . and say to them, 'The kingdom of
God has come near to you'" (Luke 10:9).

What is the kingdom? At bottom, it is the rule, the reign, the
sovereignty of God. George Ladd explains:

> Jesus said that we must "receive the kingdom of God" as little
> children (Mark 10:15). What is received? The Church? Heaven?
> What is received is God's rule. In order to enter the future
> realm of the Kingdom, one must submit himself in perfect trust
> to God's rule here and now.
>
> We must also "seek first his kingdom and his righteousness"
> (Matt. 6:33). What is the object of our quest? The Church?
> Heaven? No; we are to seek God's righteousness—His sway, His
> rule, His reign in our lives.
>
> When we pray, "Thy kingdom come," are we praying for
> heaven to come to earth? In a sense . . . but heaven is an object
> of desire only because the reign of God is to be more perfectly
> realized than it is now. . . . Therefore, what we pray for is, "Thy
> kingdom come; *thy will be done* on earth as it is in heaven." . . .
> In my church, as it is in heaven. . . . In my life, as it is in
> heaven. . . . The confidence that this prayer is to be answered
> when God brings human history to the divinely ordained con-
> summation enables the Christian to retain his balance and
> sanity of mind in this mad world in which we live.[7]

Meanwhile, as we try to understand and participate in God's
foreign policy, his plan for the peoples of the world—or even to
implement God's will locally—we are racked by the tension between the kingdom of God and the kingdom of darkness. H. R.
Rookmaaker discusses this tension:

> There is no duality between a higher and a lower, between
> grace and nature. This world is God's world. He created it, He
> sustains it, He is interested in it. He called the work of His
> hands good in the very beginning. Nothing is excluded. Every-
> thing, from the lowest atom or animal life to the highest dox-
> ology, everything belongs to Him. Nothing can exist outside of
> Him, and all things have a meaning only in relation to Him.
>
> Yet there is a sharp division—not between a realm that God
> deals with and another that is more or less autonomous, not
> between a higher and a lower, but between the kingdom, the

rule, the realm of God and the kingdom of darkness. Man, in the Fall, brought sin and, consequently, a curse into the world. And so there is a duality, between good and bad, right and wrong, beautiful and ugly. In his sinfulness man wanted to be like God, to be autonomous. And sin, bringing with it decay, sickness, and ultimately death, is still in the world, marring God's wonderful creation. This is the true division. It goes through all mankind, affecting every human being; two opposite ways, one as God wants, the other against His will. So, as Paul said, nothing is sinful, neither eating and drinking nor any kind of activity whatsoever, if done with thanksgiving. But all things are sinful if done in disobedience to God's will and Word. . . .

And so too the fact that Jesus Christ died to take upon Himself the sin of mankind is not just something for the 'soul.' The whole cosmos is to be redeemed, to be 'bought back,' for all things are under the curse of sin and evil. His saving grace, His offer of new life in all its fullness, excludes no aspect of human reality. . . .

We pray, "Thy kingdom come." We ask for God's rule to be acknowledged and extended in this life, in this world, "on earth as it is in heaven." . . . In the Old Testament . . . [God] told [his people] that they could feast with the offering of thanksgiving in the temple. . . . And He also told them that it was good to put a fence around a roof to stop people from falling off. He was anxious to give them good advice in many matters that were not simply cultic, but yet belonged to His dominion. He wanted His people to live, as He was the God of life, life in the full sense, in all human realms. He showed that nothing was excluded, neither stealing nor judging, trading nor property, sexuality nor eating and drinking. His commandments were not simply religious or ethical, they were basic principles of life. . . .

God in His wisdom knew that if His children took to other gods they were not only wrong in their faith and worship but that all life was in principle threatened—sex, politics, daily happiness. . . . And if they were reluctant to listen to the prophets, God told them that He would come with His judgment, which again was not only in matters of faith, salvation, or the afterlife, but also in this life, in their political freedom, their possessions and well-being. . . .

These great biblical principles . . . [give] an answer not only to the question of what a Christian's attitude to culture should be, but also to the question of what a Christian's attitude to a nonChristian culture should be, the very practical problem of how we are to live in a world that is full of sin and ungodliness.... Where [culture has] been spoilt or warped by sin, then the Christian must show by his life, his words, his action, his creativity, what God really intended it to be.... He is the "salt of the earth," keeping society from corruption, and giving savour to every aspect of life....

This is humanity: to make something of our life; to realize the possibilities that God has given us; to realize a good marriage, if that is for us; to do a good job, to enjoy the life one has, the possibilities laid within our personality.... Realizing one's possibilities, acting in love and freedom within given structures, fighting against sin and its results, this is what creativity means.... We are called to be creative in this sense. And to bear the cross that often goes with it, for mankind often prefers darkness to light.[8]

In relief and development work, it pays to remember that the powers of this world often prefer darkness. Take the "secular humanists" in our own society. Historically, there have been several kinds of humanists, including great Christians like Milton. More recently, the Moral Majority has nailed the word to a more narrow interpretation. To them, humanists are people who believe that man is merely the product of nature, that no Creator has endowed him with a transcendent dimension. This has implications in legal struggles over abortion. "Humanists" also refer to those who do not believe there is any permanent, revealed basis for ethics. Instead, they assume that we have within ourselves the power to develop a good society. Some humanists feel traditional Christians stand in the way of progress. Battles have erupted over pornography, abortion, contraceptives for teens, gay power, TV smut and censorship, prayer and Christian meetings in schools and other public places. Even the matter of whether religious criteria can figure in adoptions has become an issue.

This struggle should not surprise us. Given our sinful nature—since we often willfully choose what is false—it should come as no shock that the powers of this world lead us astray. This does not mean that systems or powers are evil in themselves. In fact, Colossians 1:16 tells us that the powers were created by Christ and are held together in Christ. Rather, powerful systems become evil when they usurp the central place in ordering our values and beliefs. With our tendency toward idolatry, this happens frequently.

Whether it is Marxism or sex, Islam or money, some power constantly appears on the horizon to challenge and depose Christ.

Dutch theologian Hendrik Berkhof has described the pull of the powers in his own life:

> When Hitler took the helm in Germany in 1933, the powers of Volk, race, and state took a new grip on men. Thousands were grateful, after the confusion of the preceding years, to find their lives again protected from chaos, order and security restored. No one could withhold himself, without utmost effort, from the grasp these Powers had. . . . I myself experienced almost literally how such Powers may be "in the air." . . .
>
> The state, politics, class, social struggle, national interest, public opinion, accepted morality, the ideas of decency, humanity, democracy—these give unity and direction to thousands of lives. Yet precisely by giving unity and direction, they separate these many lives from the true God: they let us believe that we have found the meaning of existence, whereas they really estrange us from true meaning.[9]

Human systems tend to take over. But Christ's death, according to 1 Corinthians 15, dethrones all powers. It does not necessarily destroy them, as some translations suggest, but it dethrones them. We Christians must follow Christ in this. As he is not only the answer to our questions but also the question posed to all our answers, so our Christian presence is also an interrogation—a continuing questioning of the legitimacy of the powers. Following Christ, who dethroned the powers, we must see them in the proper perspective, as merely one segment of creation that exists because of the Creator and is limited by other creatures. Christ rivals all powers.

What does this imply for our cross-cultural relief and development work? Does it mean withdrawing from secular institutions and establishing our own? Some Christians throughout history have thought so—persecuted early believers, medieval monastics, Leo Tolstoy, nineteenth-century missionaries who thundered that their converts must abandon all heathen ways, today's little groups of Jesus people, representatives of the counterculture. "What has Jerusalem to do with Athens?" roared the second-century apologist Tertullian. But we must take the question a step further: "What has Jerusalem to do with godliness?" This was the city that crucified our Lord. In fact, even in our own Christian institutions, power corrupts. T. S. Eliot had a wealth of biblical and historical examples to draw on when he mused,

> Servant of God has chance of greater sin
> And sorrow, than the man who serves a king.
> For those who serve the greater cause may make the cause
>   serve them,
> Still doing right: and striving with political men
> May make that cause political, not by what they do
> But by what they are.[10]

Godly men as well often make poor decisions outside their area of expertise.

Rather than withdrawing from institutions ordained by God's grace and struggling for a utopia that soon will be corrupted, we ought to be chiseling the powers that be (though sometimes the best way to do that is by building a model, like the technical school established by the society for Community Development in Pakistan, or the small businesses funded by the International Institute of Development, Inc.). Surely such efforts will bear fruit. As the song goes,

> The darkness will turn to dawning
> and the dawning to noonday bright
> and Christ's great kingdom will come on earth,
> the kingdom of love and light.

Yet our experience in history indicates, in spite of technological progress, very little moral progress. As the Christian historian Herbert Butterfield has observed,

> Each generation is . . . an end in itself, a world of people existing in their own right. . . . Every generation is equidistant from eternity. So the purpose of life is not in the far future, nor, as we so often imagine, around the next corner, but the whole of it is here and now, as fully as ever it will be on this planet. . . . [I do not know of] any mundane fullness of life which we could pretend to possess and which was not open to the people in the age of Isaiah or Plato, Dante or Shakespeare. . . . Each generation—indeed each individual—exists for the glory of God.[11]

People have been basically the same throughout recorded history. Real progress has not gone very deep.

So we have no assurance that our efforts to better societal structures will result in lasting changes. Our improved institutions may not endure. But they may make life better for some people than it would have been otherwise. That is what loving our neighbor means. We may not be responsible for the entire history of civilization. But we are responsible for caring for our neighbor, at some cost to ourselves, with all the ability that God has given us. We are to make a positive difference as the watchdogs of our communities. People of conviction in the middle of the masses. The salt of the earth. The saving remnant in our society. Deviants in the tradition of Moses, the prophets, Martin Luther, William Carey, and the abolitionists—who accomplished far more for their cultures than any conformist could have.

Love means involvement. It may mean caring enough to tell a friend he has bad breath. On the other hand, in the international arena, we must be careful about urging others to use mouthwash, realizing that foreigners often refrain from telling us about *our* strong odors. Caring cross-culturally requires special tact. In fact, in that great majority of cultures where God already has planted his church, we may expect that he will communicate through his Word and Spirit directly to local leaders. Christians must speak out against sin in other cultures. But Christians within those cultures are endowed with the resources to take the lead. We can help as models of what it means to be immersed in the Word, the Spirit, and the gripping issues of the day.

The American way is not the best way. True, to the extent that the people of a nation conform to God's moral laws, it appears that God will bless them. This preoccupied several nineteenth-century English Christian politicians, who agitated for social reforms not only out of love but also in order to preserve England's greatness. On the other hand, external conformity can be hypocritical, empty, a whitened sepulcher—and transient, disappearing in the next generation.

In any case, has America conformed to God's laws more than other nations? "America has been great because her people have been good," says Jerry Falwell of the Moral Majority, paraphrasing Alexis de Tocqueville. In *Productive Christians in an Age of Guilt Manipulators,* David Chilton makes an even stronger claim:

The "Third and Fourth Worlds" are suffering under the judgment of God. . . . An important principle is at work in history. It is this: God is continually at work to destroy unbelieving cultures and to give the world over to the dominion of His people. . . . God works to overthrow the ungodly, and increasingly the world will come under the dominion of Christians—not by military aggression, but by godly labor, saving, investment, and orientation toward the future. . . .[12]

But have Americans been appreciably nobler than the Swiss? Or, for that matter, nobler than the Indonesians, who require belief in God as one of the five points of their national creed, and who insist that every citizen be registered as a believer in some God-fearing faith?

America is not God's chosen nation. We are one among many. We may be the joggers in God's park. Other peoples may be flexible gymnasts. Others may be sweating out a fierce game of handball. Taken all together, we make the park exciting.

God's foreign policy intends this rich complementary diversity. He has designed a mosaic of all peoples and tribes and kindreds and nations to sparkle around his throne. The kingdom of God is not a castration of cultural uniqueness. All one in Christ does not mean colorless uniformity.

This conviction is put to the test when we come up against foreign nationalism. How should we react? Nationalism can be idolatry. We remember Hitler's Germany. Zambian churchmen recently have put together a careful document warning against the excesses of nationalism. Zimbabwe's new Black bishop cautions against it. We see the dangers in our own tendency to embrace civil religion, our pride in putting America first. Yet, properly limited, nationalistic ideologies are important incentives for nurturing the stewardship of distinct cultural traditions. "Is nationalism a friend or foe of the Gospel?" William Girao asks in an article by that title. He answers:

Nationalism is imbedded in the Scriptures. As the chosen people of God, Israel was fiercely nationalistic. The Psalms are replete with nationalistic sentiments. The Prophets were messengers primarily concerned for Israel and Judah (Isa. 1:1; Jer. 4:5; Ez. 2:3). They identified passionately with their people (Neh. 1:5-6).

Nationalism is in the New Testament. The Lord Jesus Himself identified with the Jews. They were "his own" (John 1:11). He was sent to Israel first and primarily (Matt. 15:23-28). He dedicated his public ministry to the Jews, and rarely reached beyond them.

Although Paul held Roman citizenship, he was proud to be a "Hebrew of the Hebrews." Of course he considered this less than nothing when compared with identification with Christ (Phil. 3:5, 8). But in fact Paul loved his own people so much that he was willing to go to hell if that would bring them to Christ (Rom. 9:3-5). . . .

The brain drain is not a rhetorical device. Every year our [Philippine] churches' most crucial lay leaders go abroad. Many choose never to return.

When Filipinos leave the Philippines rather than stay and help bail it out of its problems, something is drastically wrong with our society and also with those who are leaving. Nationalism draws us back where we belong—to our home, where our leadership is most needed. . . .

Nationalism is the foundation of internationalism. The self-respect and the sense of dignity and worth fostered by nationalism challenge us to try the more complicated task of witnessing to people of a different culture. This merging of national strains, when based on distinct national identities, results in an authentic fellowship in diversity rather than a hypocritical fellowship of conformity. . . .

Is nationalism a friend or foe of the gospel? Nationalism is a friend, an ally in our evangelizing and discipling. But like any other abstraction, nationalism may be misunderstood. Like any other popular movement, it will draw false followers. Like any love it can be perverted.

Should we repudiate nationalism because we are afraid of the risks? We would have to reject many other necessary movements and abstract realities—even the idea of love itself, since love has so often been abused, misunderstood, and made an excuse for countless crimes.

I maintain that as a nationalist I can serve God better.[13]

National loyalty matters. In Latin America, according to René Padilla, while church growth is remarkable, its loss of members is appalling. As fast as converts enter the front doors, young people slip out the back. Why? For lack of biblical grounding—and also because they cannot see how their faith relates to their roots.

In Pakistan, the admirable Society for Community Development, which trains young men in marketable technical skills, appears to lack one thing: teaching about Christian nationalism, the stewardship of their own culture. And SCD's center does not focus on the landless urban masses who so desperately need employment: though it accepts all needy applicants, it has a bias toward rural areas. Yet its graduates don't return home. Many take jobs in cities. Others travel to the Middle East, where employers clamor for Pakistani labor and pay ten times as much as bosses in Pakistan.

So the home communities receive foreign exchange, but they lose ability and initiative. It's not an equal trade. Poor communities don't need money so much as they need wise, motivated local leadership.

We can understand why the young graduates may not feel strongly motivated to go where it will help their country most. Pakistan has been torn apart by ethnic hatreds. In 1947, when India was granted independence and Pakistan came into existence, twelve million Hindu, Muslim, and Sikh refugees fled past each other across the new India-Pakistan border. When refugees met, they massacred each other. In a few months, over 250,000 people had been slaughtered. In view of this, the SCD graduate may well think to himself, "Pakistan needs me. But the question is, do I need Pakistan?"

Unquestionably, for a Pakistani to become a Christian businessman in a small town is no easy task. Studies indicate that ninety-nine percent of the small grocery stores and shops that SCD's graduates might aspire to run will fail within a year. For Christians, ostracized from many powerful networks, both the challenges of accumulating capital and collecting bills loom as huge obstacles. In light of this, an SCD graduate might well be advised to work in the Middle East for a few years—to save a nest egg, to hone his skills, to broaden his knowledge of the world, to mature. Whereas he could barely support himself by working at home, he can support his whole extended family by working in Dubai—educate his brothers and sisters, buy his parents a better home, get his family out of debt. Nevertheless, eventually he should plan to come home, to benefit not only his family but also his community and nation.

SCD needs to teach students Christian stewardship of their own culture. And more of SCD's graduates need to become Christian entrepreneurs in their home regions.

God's world is enriched by diversity. Social reparation is a commendable goal, but we Americans must back our concern for social justice with our appreciation of different cultures. Caring doesn't mean patronizing the poor and destroying their cultures. We must not only see others' needs; we must also admire their strengths. In fact, we can't serve them unless we appreciate how their differences enrich us.

Black is not beautiful if we follow the ideas of William Shockley. But in Christ, Black is beautiful. So is White. So is multi-ethnic American. Praise God for our culture. We don't need to be ashamed of it. Praise God for our bodies—tall, strong, clean, unscarred—the result of plenty of food and good health care. For our frankness, friendliness, energy, confidence, determination to succeed. For our belief that every man has the right to his own opinion, however misguided. Praise God for cheap ice cream, hot running water, computers, and painless dentistry.

At the same time, let's remember that every culture is the lifeway of people made in the image of God, regardless of their standard of living. Most people with whom God has communicated throughout history have lived in cultures far different from ours. Was Noah literate? Did David believe in democracy? Did Mary have indoor plumbing? Probably no—yet their lives were as valid as ours. They dominated nature less. Fewer alternative products, customs, and ideas were available to them. But they experienced friendship, love, parenthood, creativity, learning, responsibility, choice, dignity, adventure, and a relationship to God. They had as many significant experiences as any modern Western person.

Sin is present in other cultures, but it's in our culture, too. And so are God's gifts. So let's share them. Maybe we have something to teach others about hygiene or individual responsibility. Maybe we have something to learn from others about hospitality or respect for our elders. Let's investigate how we can praise our King as a community of diversity.

1. Karl Menninger, *Whatever Became of Sin?* (New York: Hawthorne Books, 1973), p. 188.
2. Alexander Schmemann, "Solzhenitsyn," *Radix*, March 1974, p. 11.
3. Erich Sauer, *The King of the Earth* (Grand Rapids, Mich.: Eerdmans, 1962), p. 81.

4. H. R. Rookmaaker, *Modern Art and the Death of Culture* (London: Inter-Varsity Press, 1970), p. 36.

5. Bob Dylan, "Saved," *Slow Train Coming*, Columbia, 36120, 1980.

6. This discussion of the kingdom is based upon George Ladd's *The Gospel of the Kingdom* (Grand Rapids, Mich.: Eerdmans, 1954).

7. *Ibid.*, pp. 21-23.

8. Rookmaaker, *Modern Art and the Death of Culture*, pp. 36-38.

9. Hendrik Berkhof, *Christ and the Powers* (Scottdale, Pa.: Herald Press, 1962), pp. 32-33.

10. T. S. Eliot, *Murder in the Cathedral* (New York: Harcourt, Brace and World, 1935), p. 45.

11. Herbert Butterfield, *Christianity and History* (London: Fontana Books, 1957), pp. 89, 91.

12. David Chilton, *Productive Christians in an Age of Guilt Manipulators: A Biblical Response to Ron Sider* (Tyler, Tex.: Institute for Christian Economics, 1981), pp. 78-79.

13. William Girao, "Is Nationalism a Friend or Foe of the Gospel?" in *The Message, Men, and Mission* (Manila, the Philippines: Inter-Varsity Christian Fellowship, 1971), pp. 80-86.

CHAPTER 7

AMERICAN ALTERNATIVES
Where to Begin

Jon Meeser designs cardiology instruments. Remember those stationary bicycles attached to stress monitors? Jon designs both the software and the hardware for them. With a wife and a baby, and in the market for a house, Jon has heavy expenses. But he pulls down a decent salary as an engineer.

With this salary, Jon and his wife Ariel help support Chavannes Jeune in Haiti. Here, where a quarter of the children are woefully underfed, Chavannes helps administer a development program that promotes health care, better marketing networks, small industries, literacy programs, and general adult education through radio. Here, where the government's dread secret police, the Tonton Macoute, rule the countryside, and where the cruelty of district bureaucrats usually goes unchecked, Christians in this development program have fought back by organizing massive offerings of prayer and by persistently hammering away at injustice through legal channels. Here, where voodoo enslaves people, where sorcerers claim to be able to turn people into zombies, dozens of churches associated with the development program demonstrate that the spirit of Christ is stronger than any other spirit. They show that Christ's death frees us from the grip of the powers of darkness.

All this is possible partly because Jon and Ariel give. As a matter of fact, these young people, scraping together the down payment for their first mortgage, have quietly determined to share twenty-five percent of their income. And they do.

How? For the first fourteen months of their married life, Jon and Ariel eked out an existence on $225 a month as managers of a motel—and tuition for graduate school came out of that. Later, when they both got good jobs, they decided to continue without a car. Jon jogs five miles to work. Ariel and baby Gabrielle get around by bus. The Meesers also decided to spend no more than fifteen dollars a week for groceries, and five dollars a week for household supplies. Throughout most of the 1970's they kept to that budget.

Jon and Ariel relish homemade soups. They patronize the "seconds" shop of Oberto's Sausage for inexpensive pizza toppings. They get books and magazines from libraries. For furniture, they began with a crate for a table (around which they knelt to eat), a rocking chair, and a desk—and since then have "made use of the overabundance of other people."

"One of the secrets is not having time to shop," Jon says. They share time as lavishly as they share money. A Ph.D. student has a serious problem with procrastination? To keep her accountable, Jon and Ariel regularly will spend two big blocks of time with her every week. A large mission conference needs a myriad of details coordinated? Busy young parents, Jon and Ariel have been active workers in four such conferences, and have completely coordinated two. And they find numerous other ways to serve. Developing a puppet show on world hunger and presenting it at churches. Pushing through piles of papers in missionary mailings. "Being aware when a family with small kids is moving . . . being there to help . . . not waiting till they call you. . . ." Evaluating mission projects so that they balance their giving to both local and international evangelism, and both local and international relief and development, all programs having little overhead and good track records. Who has time to shop? The Meesers also spend time and money employing acquaintances who are temporarily out of work as babysitters or as "mother's helpers"—at a good hourly wage.

"It's not a sense of discipline or a constant vision before us," says Jon. "It's just force of habit. We don't spend money on ourselves. We put giving at the top of the list."

Jon's parents are conservative financially. They don't go into debt, and they don't spend money on things they don't need. Ariel's family never throws anything away. Instead, they "make do." Creatively. In the middle of Jon and Ariel's apartment is a magnificent eight-foot-long peacock redwood coffee table inlaid with shells and driftwood—an original by Ariel's dad.

When Jon was in grade school, his mother began a school class for handicapped children. That helped Jon choose to work at a job in medical technology rather than at a better-paying job designing military equipment at Boeing. Eventually Jon hopes to design mobility and communications systems for children who have cerebral palsy.

Meanwhile, he and Ariel aim to make their "long-range investment in the kingdom of God which will last forever—not in retirement benefits which will last just a few years." They want to "invest in people—because a lot can be done with people with just a few resources."

"Love your neighbor." What does that mean internationally in this Reagan era? Several suggestions have been made in this book:

- that community development in the Third World is obedience to biblical teaching.
- that it can be a sound, successful investment. We don't have to throw our money away. We can learn to identify projects that work, projects that make sense, projects that have a good chance of success.
- that community development can be a fascinating adventure.
- that we, through prayer and through personal or church giving, can be part of this without leaving home.

Jon and Ariel illustrate how an American family can rearrange priorities to participate in this outreach.

In one sense this book is for medical, agricultural, business, and general community development workers in poor countries. But in another sense it is for us lay Christians who stay home and support them. We too are called to increase God's kingdom. And we are called to do this wisely.

What are the implications for our lives in America?

Above my desk is a motto: "Writing is planned neglect." But all significant living is planned neglect. As the Chinese philosopher Mencius said long ago, "Before a man can do things, there must be things he will not do." Certainly, if we want to be part of the battle for God's kingdom, if we want to help implement God's foreign policy, if we want to be pilgrims rather than tourists,[1] there are things to which we must say "No." Good things. In our home life as well as our business life, we cannot simply go along with the crowd. We must make choices.

In her book entitled *You Can Be the Wife of a Happy Husband*—a book which contains many biblical and useful ideas—Darien Cooper has devised a planning wheel called "The Balanced Activities of the Wife." The categories on the wheel include "husband," "homemaking," "children," "appearance," "money and security," "in-laws," and "outside activities." Cooper has included a long passage of personal beauty tips. A whole section on how to decorate your bedroom attractively. She advises that you try a new menu each week, even if your family is suspicious of new foods.[2]

All well and good. But are these the things that really matter?

If we thought about the abused children in our own city—and if we were aware that there are programs through which we and our children could spend one to ten hours a week with an abusive mother and her children—would it matter if we served the same menu every week? Unless one of your special gifts is cooking, new menus can be satanic. They can blind you to real needs.

If we were aware of the vast needs of refugee immigrants—their needs for conversation partners, for jobs as housecleaners, gardeners, seamstresses, for friends—maybe we would think less about redecorating our bedrooms and more about serving these people.

If we were aware that even in a small city like Seattle there are probably about three thousand Muslims, probably sixty Muslim women, we might spend less time at parties where we can sample cosmetics, buy Tupperware, and learn what colors to wear, and more time and energy where the real action is.

If we were aware of the needs and opportunities for community development in poor countries. . . .

If we were aware that we could influence multinational corporations to function more justly. . . .

How often we housewives act as though our energies didn't matter to the world. Perhaps we women are not raised with a sufficient consciousness of battle. Consequently, we are at ease while the world burns.

Certainly there is a time for creating a tranquil oasis where our family and friends can be refreshed. But there is also a time to march.

Catherine Booth was co-founder of the Salvation Army. When she had four children, the eldest age four, she began to preach. Her husband had just left his salaried position as pastor to become an unpaid evangelist in the slums. Catherine continued preaching, even though over the next several years she had four more children. When she traveled as an evangelist, all eight of them often traveled with her. Those were the times she would arrive at her destinations complete with children, nursery furniture, and a big rug—so that her children wouldn't ruin the carpets in the homes where she stayed!

Catherine frequently addressed two or three thousand people at a single meeting—uneducated, disruptive people of the slums. At the end of the meetings she counseled those who came forward—no large organization like Billy Graham's behind her. After that she struggled to find jobs for all the newly reformed prostitutes and pickpockets. For years to come she would correspond with them. Beyond this, Catherine tried whenever possible to devote one evening a week to visiting the families of alcoholics.

She had one assistant, a woman more like a sister than a servant, who stayed with the Booths all her life, although they rarely could pay her. One helper, for those eight sets of diapers, without any washer or dryer, in rainy England. Catherine and her assistant made all the children's clothes until the children were twelve years old. What kind of mother was Catherine? Her letters to her children pulsate with the painstaking, individual thought she gave to each child.

At the same time (and without a word processor, either!), she managed to write eight books.

Catherine Booth understood that she was fighting a battle for the kingdom of God.[3]

Several years ago, Karen Mains, author of *Open Heart, Open Home,* found herself in the middle of redecorating an old inner-city house. Her home vibrated with life and giving. Innumerable guests found warmth, gracious, intelligent conversation—and even a relationship with God—in those surroundings. Karen wanted to serve them. And in a run-down, crime-ridden neighborhood, she wanted to demonstrate how to create beauty on a limited budget.

But one day she sat down and calculated that this redecorating would absorb her energies for the next two years. Meanwhile, she was feeling somewhat out of touch with God. That day she rearranged her priorities. She relegated redecorating to the sidelines. Beyond that, she determined not to enter any store but a grocery store for three months—and not to read anything but the Bible until it came alive to her![4]

Karen has never regretted those choices.

In her book, *Women at the Crossroads,* Kari Torjesen Malcolm describes her mother, a Norwegian missionary to China. She

records the song that she and her sisters and brothers sang while
they waited in the afternoon for their mother to return from her
teaching:

> Mamma's coming home soon
> Mamma's coming home soon
> Mamma's coming home soon
> I am glad.

Kari's parents took turns caring for their children because they
believed they both had pivotal ministries. Years later, when Kari
was hiding passively behind her husband's ministry and feeling
run-down and depressed, her mother chided, "Of course. What do
you expect?" Kari explains, "My mother thought I should be out of
the house, evangelizing the world and using all my God-given gifts
to help others. As a nurse and a Christian, she believed very
strongly that if we are not doing what God intends us to be doing,
we will get sick."

For the past twenty years, Kari and her husband have both
enjoyed vigorous ministries, following her mother's advice.[5]

It is not that we Christian women in America spend our time in
blatant maliciousness; it is just that we spend so much time "pouring sand down ratholes," to use John Alexander's terminology.[6]

Just as our home life needs to be arranged so that we can fight
the real battles, so do our business priorities. Of course we have to
make a profit. Otherwise we'll go out of business, and our family,
employees, creditors, colleagues, and many others will suffer. In
these tough times, just breaking even may consume a great deal of
energy. Yet questions of priorities remain—and they go beyond
what is legal or illegal. They concern how justly we make our
profit, even within the bounds of the law, and how justly it is
distributed. These are kingdom questions. We cannot facilitate
justice elsewhere unless we practice it at home. If we do not, we
may not even be able to recognize what is needed elsewhere.

A few years ago, William Krutza interviewed two hundred men
who called themselves Christian businessmen.

"What do you mean when you say you're a Christian businessman?" he asked them.

"I've accepted Christ as my Savior," most of them answered. "I
trust in his death and resurrection—"

"But—how do you relate Christianity to business?"

By having a Bible on the desk. Using religious mottos on letterheads or in ads. Encouraging employees to hold Bible studies (during their own lunch hours). Praying before meeting clients. Doing some public speaking, which usually didn't go beyond telling when and where they "received Jesus Christ as their personal Savior." These were some of the responses.

What more could these businessmen do to relate their faith to their work? Krutza makes several suggestions. They could try to think as Christians about some of the basic issues raised by their professions. Limiting their own competitiveness. Maintaining good employee relations. Hiring people who are job risks, like ex-prisoners. Making an equitable profit. Making essential products, rather than those that encourage people to become increasingly materialistic. Creating ecologically sound products.[7]

Our business priorities, like our home lives, need to be streamlined for the kingdom.

In the introduction we stumbled into a minefield of objections to helping the poor. Aren't the world's needs too big for us to tackle? Shouldn't we focus on evangelism rather than economics? Shouldn't we work out America's economic problems first?

We answered, in the words of Jesus to the disciples of John the Baptist, "Come and see."

What, then, have we seen in our jog through the topics of health care, agriculture, small businesses, political organization, refugee assistance, and a theology of culture? Have we detonated any mines?

"IT'S HOPELESS"

We flip on the TV in the evening. Poland is in political upheaval. There are serious food shortages. Lebanon is exploding with problems: orphans, medical needs, a destroyed infrastructure, hunger. Mexico's economy is in a shambles: more desperate wetbacks cross the Rio Grande every week. East Africa suffers from serious famine. In crafts that are barely boats, refugees bob toward a better life somewhere, coming not only from Indochina but also from Haiti. El Salvador is a powder keg. Guatemala has many maimed, uprooted, frightened, needy people.

We flip off the TV. What can we do about all that? We can't even understand it. The world is too complex. Its needs are too big.

And too regular. As soon as we send a little money to plug up one hole, another hole gapes somewhere else. Magazines from Christian agencies feed us constant hype. Each month's disaster is the worst the director has ever seen, as he stumbles, jet-lagged, microphone in hand, among orphans with bloated bellies.

Our books on the subject are not much more optimistic. In a famous study, the international Club of Rome has predicted that pollution, depletion of nonrenewable resources, population growth, and economic growth will lay waste the world by the year 2025. Of course, this is balanced by the Institute for Food and Development Policy, which argues that enough food is produced right now to feed every person adequately, and by others who argue that science soon will develop renewable sources of energy.

At any rate, our mass of knowledge inoculates us against action. We can't send money to every huckster, however worthy his cause. Surely that's not what Christ meant when he said, "Give to him who asks of you."

So we flip off the TV. Do we lift Lebanon up to the Lord in prayer? Do we commend Poland to the One who is the rightful ruler of that geography and those people? Do we intercede quietly for wisdom in handling Mexican wetbacks and Haitian and Salvadoran refugees in a way that will also be fair to U. S. citizens?

Or do we instead turn from the TV and pull out our datebooks, scheming how to fit another event into our busy schedules? Or lie back and dream about a new video game or jogging shoes? Or pick up the sports page? Or a historical novel? As for our money, since the world's needs are too big, we spend it on a home computer. Cross-country skiing. A Hawaiian vacation. Or an addition to the church.

Yet when we, with all our knowledge—however superficial—of the world, make no response to world events, we deny Christ's lordship over them. True, disasters never stop occurring. True, no individual, no church, no denomination can help out in every crisis. True, we often give ignorantly, and our gifts often are distributed corruptly. Does that give us the right to flip off the TV like atheists?

Mary Slessor was an uneducated Scottish "mill lassie" who believed God wanted her in West Africa in the late 1800's. She sailed there, and put down roots.

In Calabar, where she lived, her mission had a death rate of one missionary per year. Those who survived were regularly bedridden with malarial fever. That was part of the job description —if you were lucky.

Like all foreign women, Mary soon lost her beauty. But she was not inhibited. In this region where three centuries of slave trading had disrupted relatively egalitarian farming societies and had precipitated the development of cruel, inhumane, despotic empires, Mary went her way alone. Since her Victorian bustles and veils caught on the trail bushes, she discarded them and began wearing "shameless" simple cotton dresses. When she was sixty, Mary learned to ride that new invention, the bicycle—over rough trails, naturally. She immersed herself in African law, and eventually, as the only Britisher who dared to live in some hostile areas, she was appointed Vice-Consul to the Okoyong—the first woman granted such a post in the whole of the British Empire.

Mary was an evangelist, a medical worker, and an educator. She is known particularly for coming to the rescue of dozens of babies and women condemned to die. On the trail or in the regal courtroom, her babies were always with her. Suffering from malaria and threatened by human and animal danger, complex cultural and litigational tangles, and, it must be admitted, the mission's intransigence, Mary persevered. She rocked her babies at night by devising a unique system: she suspended each one in a cradle-hammock made from a tinned-milk crate, tied a string to each crate, and as she lay in bed, pulled the right string as each infant needed soothing. To bathe her babies, she would put four big milk tins on the stove to warm the water, plop in four babies, wash them, take them out and dry them, plop in four more—all the time discussing points of law with those who sought an audience with her. In Africa, Mary became known as *Eka Kpukpro Owo,* Mother of All Peoples.[8]

Mary Slessor is by no means unique. Bartolome de las Casas lobbied almost single-handedly against the slavery and incredible death-rate of Indians working in the tin and silver mines and on the plantations and haciendas in Latin America. He felt he must speak out if he was to be consistent with God's law and God's love. Pandita Ramabai graciously, assertively, and untiringly opened alternatives for Indian women. The love of Christ motivated her. William Wilberforce gave twenty years of his life to outlaw the slave trade. The world's needs are too big? Throughout the centuries, when times have been bleak, Christians moved by love for people and a commitment to stewardship of God's world have tackled bad conditions.

But not blindly. In this book we have suggested some criteria and safeguards for increasing the success of our projects. At the same time, knowing that disasters never disappear should make us more humble. Rather than expecting success, rather than smothering the poor with cheap cheerfulness, we may at times need to sit silently with them, to empathize, to share our mutual lack of answers. And then, to our surprise, we may discover that they have unexpected coping resources. Gold jewelry may come out of hiding. Rich acquaintances may be tapped. More parts of locally grown plants may be discovered to be nutritious. Knowing that disasters never disappear, then, should rein in our naive optimism. Nevertheless, we dare not ignore the world that the news media have so deeply imprinted on our minds. While we cannot do everything, we Christians have many more networking resources available today than did Mary Slessor or William Wilberforce. For our own sakes as well as for the sake of God's world, we dare not shrug it off.

"EVANGELISM IS OUR FOCUS"

"'[Alleviating world hunger] is an individual issue,'" explains Moral Majority stalwart Tim LaHaye. "'The real question is, Are you helping people most by giving them bread to eat? Or by leading them to a vital life-changing experience with Jesus Christ and then showing them how to become self-sufficient?

"'I have visited the Setewel Indians on the southern tip of Mexico. They were a vanishing group until some missionaries went there 25 years ago. Today, as a result, they are the most productive Indian tribe in Mexico. They have been transformed by the power of Christ. Here were a people who were starving and now they are self-respecting, productive and effective.'"[9]

All people, at whatever physical level—refugees adrift with nothing but the rags on their backs, peasant farmers eking out a bare existence, or residents of a condominium on Chicago's North Shore—need Christ. Raising people's standard of living is superficial. Ultimately it will not meet their deepest human needs. It will not give them the abundant life that they were created for.

Many philanthropists help poor people economically. But we

can help at a much deeper level. We can help with the gospel of Jesus Christ. We must direct our focus here.

Is it really *evangelism* that is the opposite of economic help? Isn't it rather responsible *consumerism* that is the opposite? If we limited our self-centered spending, wouldn't we have resources for both evangelistic service and material aid? How much money are we spending on remodeling our homes? How much time? How much are we spending on recreation? Or on a good music system? John White has spoken of "murder by hairspray." Art Beals has talked of "pornographic food." While many Filipino pastors have fewer than thirty books, we have "dress for success" articles for pastors. While poverty ages millions of Filipino women before their time—whether they are peasants, urban seamstresses, or piecework assemblers of electronic components employed by our multinationals—we have Patricia French's Christian Charm and Modeling Schools, which affirm, "Christian women should be as glamorous and beautiful as they want to be."

Speaking at Wheaton College on the topic "Why Am I Unhappy as a Professional Scientist?" a few years ago, John Brobeck answered himself, ". . . the answer is that I have lived most of my life in a state of frustration, because so many scientific discoveries raise philosophical and moral problems that seem to me to be terribly urgent, and because I am unable to persuade friends who are Christians to try to answer them. . . ."[10]

Among the many questions Brobeck raises are these:

> For two thousand years Christians have known the truth of Jesus' saying, "Your neighbors will know you are my disciples by the way you live." . . . I confess that if I meet someone at dinner and note that he orders a double martini, that while waiting for the first course to be served he lights a cigarette, and that he uses profanity in our conversation, I may wonder whether or not he is a fellow Christian. Likewise . . . can you entertain the suggestion that a Christian is one who vacations in a sailboat rather than a powerboat, and skis cross country rather than with a tow? One who does not own a golf cart, nor a snowmobile, nor possibly even a power mower? A person who rides a bicycle for transportation as well as for recreation; whose car has a well-tuned 1200 cc. motor? Finally, and most important, who controls his own food intake so that his body weight is reduced to, and remains at, a level five to ten per cent

below standard American values for his age and height? . . .
Have you considered what might happen if every Christian
in this country lived merely according to the outline I just
sketched?[11]

Is *evangelism* the opposite of economic help? Isn't it rather
responsible *consumerism?*

Suppose we ran a day-care center for children. We would wipe
noses. We would teach children to sing and count and dress themselves. We might well teach them John 3:16. We would also report
child abuse, and possibly even try to change social structures to
protect children we had come to care for. Love doesn't compart-
mentalize. Similarly, love for our brothers doesn't distinguish between spiritual and physical bread.

The apostle James has written, "My brothers, what use is it for a
man to say he has faith when he does nothing to show it? Can that
faith save him? Suppose a brother or a sister is in rags with
not enough food for the day, and one of you says, 'Good luck to
you, keep yourselves warm, and have plenty to eat,' but does
nothing to supply their bodily needs, what is the good of that? So
with faith: if it does not lead to action, it is in itself a lifeless thing"
(2:14-17 NEB).

We Americans dash from Bible study to handball court to board
room to exercise class to beauty parlor, yet we sing, "This World Is
Not My Home." We say, "Doesn't the Bible say the world is going
to have to get worse and worse before Jesus comes?"—and then
we sit down and plan long-term investments for ourselves, and
design church buildings guaranteed to last fifty years.

This world is the Lord's, and we do well to affirm it. But when
we spend so much effort on preserving our material possessions
and our physical bodies, shouldn't we care for the basic physical
well-being of God's other children?

"WE HAVE TO TACKLE
AMERICA'S ECONOMIC PROBLEM FIRST"

"America is great because America is good," Alexis de Tocqueville
wrote after his famous tour of the young nation. Many still believe
that. Haven't we led the struggle toward a democratic form of
government? Haven't we, along with Europe, given modern medicine to the rest of mankind? By our inventions and efficiency,

haven't we raised the whole world's standard of living? By demonstrating the success of an egalitarian, self-help spirit, haven't we motivated many people to tackle their own problems more vigorously? And aren't we a generous people, since we contribute almost two billion dollars a year in private foreign aid?

Don't we deserve financial blessing? The Old Testament overflows with verses which tie wealth to godly living. Of the righteous man, Psalm 1:3 tells us, "whatever he does will prosper." In Isaiah 48:17, God identifies himself as "the Lord your God, who teaches you to profit. . . ." Our cultural heroes—Abraham, David, and Job—were made wealthy by God.

So today can we not expect God to bless us financially? "Yes," says Zig Ziglar in *See You at the Top*. "Yes," says David Chilton in *Productive Christians in an Age of Guilt Manipulators*. "Yes," says Gloria Copeland in *God's Will Is Prosperity*. "'Satan cannot stop the flow of God's financial blessings. . . . Redemption from the curse of poverty is part of Jesus' substitutionary work at Calvary,'" says Copeland.[12]

Therefore, especially in a recession such as we are experiencing as I write this in 1982, we must focus first on our own financial needs and on our own national economy. After all, if we don't provide for the needs of our own household first, we are worse than infidels (1 Tim. 5:8). And how can we love others until we love ourselves? As Richard DeVos, founder of Amway, says, "'To love others as myself, I must first think well of myself. . . . We are worthy people who should stand tall, talk and walk straight, be proud of what we are. . . . Then I can love someone else as I love myself.'"[13]

It is a matter of degree. We must provide for our own needs, or how will we be able to help others? "Let the thief no longer steal, but rather let him labor, doing honest work with his hands, so that he may be able to give to those in need" (Eph. 4:28). But do our own *needs* include a brand-name winter wardrobe, a new car, and all sorts of educational enrichments before we can think of the simple starvation, or the dead-end opportunities, of brothers overseas?

In Chapter Four I cited Stephen Monsma's argument that while we must consider the needs of American citizens first, we must not conduct America's business in such a cutthroat way that the citizens of other nations are harmed. He applies this specifically to international trade practices.

Like Abraham, we are to be those through whom all nations are blessed. Like Isaiah envisioned, we are to be light to the nations. Like the apostle John, we are to delight in the flourishing of all peoples and tongues and kindreds and nations, to God's glory. How can we do this when we live in comfort and they live in pain?

Of course God wants us to be rich. Lands, bustling international trade, silks, jewels, cosmetics, rich foods—the Scripture revels in all of that. We are to be rich. But not while God's other children are ragged. We are interdependent. Even if this were not true morally, it would be true practically. We have to import bauxite to make aluminum. We have to import uranium to run our nuclear plants. We have to import oil. We are interdependent. Like it or not, we are plugged into the rest of the world. Certainly God wants us to profit, but this is not his most basic teaching. Jesus' basic command is, "Love God, and love your neighbor."

"I GOTTA SPREAD BARK DUST"

Jon and Ariel are alert to the world's problems because the love of Christ constrains them, because they see that we take from the rest of the world, and because they believe that we can do *something* significant to help.

The opposite of economic assistance, they believe, is not evangelism but responsible consumerism. We are not limited so much by hopelessness as by compartmentalization—the separation between us, the winners, and "them," the losers.

Believing this, Jon and Ariel have rearranged their priorities. They limit their spending on themselves and maximize their investment in evangelism, relief programs, and development projects.

All of us in the United States face this challenge. Not first of all to give money. Some of us are struggling to pay basic monthly bills. Money is not always what the poor need, anyway. The real challenge is to give ourselves—through prayer, through curiosity and the procurement of relevant information, and through making contact with Christians and worthwhile development projects in other lands, and with Christians in our own communities who can offer us mutual support—and then, as we have opportunity, the challenge is to give money wisely. Ultimately, the challenge for us American Christians is to focus on kingdom priorities.

Marlene is a friend of mine who jogs. She can't understand

people who sag around in flabby bodies, watching TV, fixing this and that, chatting on the telephone, snacking—never knowing the exhilaration of being in shape.

"The other day I asked my neighbor if he wanted to run with me, and you know what he said?" she confided to me indignantly.

"What?"

"He said, 'I'd sure like to run today, Marlene—but I gotta spread bark dust. . . .'" Marlene snorted. Bark dust versus the joy of speed and the vigor of health! She shook her head.

The kingdom of God is far more thrilling than running, and far more lasting than a trim body. Yet how many of us postpone deep involvement until we get our bark dust spread—or some other equivalent task done?

"Before a man can do things, there must be things he will not do."

How can we support more effective projects? In this book we have indicated ways to do that. Development that is integrated—not compartmentalized—is a necessity: health care must be buttressed by food production; food production must be buttressed by nonagricultural job creation; job creation must be buttressed by political consciousness-raising and organized efforts pressing for more just-opportunity systems, especially in the ownership of land and decision-making structures. Such political consciousness-raising can be local, national, or international. While one missionary cannot do all of this for a city of eight million, he can be part of a consortium tackling it in fellowship.

Anthropology should be part of our arsenal of approaches. Culture reveals a people's deep identity. It reveals who they are in time and space in the universe. If treated lightly, cultural differences will erupt at awkward junctures. Anthropology helps by reminding us of the systematic interrelationship between behaviors; the functions of behaviors as well as their forms; real as well as ideal behaviors; group as well as individual behaviors; both nature and history as important influences on structured behaviors.

Anthropologists ask significant questions. Is the project expressed in local concepts that make sense? Is it compatible with local values? Is it compatible with local social structures? Is it economically feasible? Is it expressed through attractive local media? Is it reinforced through local festivities and celebrations?

Regarding values, are we allowing for different work rhythms? Different expectations about how long negotiations will take? Different socialization patterns? Our competitiveness versus others' group orientation? Our individualism versus others' tendency to reduce assets by sharing with relatives? Our emphasis on personal success versus others' emphasis on family pride or ethnic or national liberation? Our efficiency versus others' more relaxed and diffuse approach? Our emphasis on youth, modernity, and progress versus others' emphasis on age and tradition?

Regarding social structures, are we aware of different leadership networks? Different decision-making patterns? Different ways of settling quarrels? Have we identified segments of the population who feel that they need what is being offered? Who feel that they will gain more than they will lose if they change? Who have hope, and the power to make decisions? Have we located opinion leaders and important symbolic figures, both local and national? To foster group cohesiveness, are we acquainted with the rights and obligations of members of a given group; any distinctive roles; special rituals or celebrations; myths or the special reputation of the group; models; villains; other techniques of boundary maintenance; any distinctions between formal and informal behavior?

Regarding economic resources, can we adjust to an irregular supply of power? To irregular transportation and communication networks? To equipment with parts that are replaceable in the country at low cost? To simplified accounting? To labor-intensive procedures, using minimal automated equipment? Are we fostering the production of essentials—inexpensive food, low-cost housing, intermediate technology—rather than nonessentials? Are we marketing to the poor rather than to global islands of the rich? Are we encouraging entrepreneurs to maintain simple lifestyles, and to themselves provide progressive opportunities for workers, such as some degree of profit sharing?

Regarding communication styles, do we take into consideration our frankness versus many others' more indirect and euphemistic expression? Can we accept the common use of intermediaries in disputes? Can we adjust to the need for multiple repetitions and much longer time for successful communication in some countries? Are we sensitive to different body language?

All this is buttressed by our theology of culture. We believe God has showered gifts of his common grace on every culture in which we work. God has made these people in his image—thus they can make responsible decisions about their future. Secular community developers want people to "own" a project, because this enormously enhances success. We, however, have not only pragmatic reasons but also theological reasons for working with and under local people as they take charge.

When overpopulation discourages us, it helps to know that people who feel economically secure are the ones who tend to seek out information about family planning and to limit the number of their children. When the corruption of the elite or the inefficiency of the poor discourage us, it helps to know—especially when we work through the local church—that the Word and the Spirit which convict us also stand as guideposts for them, enabling them to become increasingly loving and just, as increasingly they are conformed to God's image through Jesus Christ. There are supracultural standards: there is a transcendent basis for optimism, for hope.

To work genuinely with local people requires the nitty-gritty anthropological method of "participant observation." It means living with them, traveling on public vehicles with them, playing with them, praying with them more than with our foreign colleagues, reading their magazines more than *Time,* and eventually internalizing the cultural symbols that can unleash torrents of motivation within them.

Which is more significant: to immerse ourselves in a local community, being sensitive to its values, or to restructure national and international political and economic systems? Community developers argue this question. Actually, both strategies are essential to holistic development.

E. C. Banfield, author of *The Moral Basis of a Backward Society,* has contended that the poor do not need economic opportunities so much as they need changed values:

> So long as the city contains a sizable lower class, nothing basic can be done about its most serious problems. Good jobs may be offered to all, but some will remain chronically unemployed. Slums may be demolished, but if the housing that replaces them is occupied by the lower class it will shortly be turned into new slums. Welfare payments may be doubled or tripled and a negative income tax instituted, but some persons

will continue to live in squalor and misery. New schools may be
built, new curricula devised, and the teacher-pupil ratio cut in
half, but if the children who attend these schools come from
lower-class homes, the schools will be turned into blackboard
jungles, and those who graduate or drop out from them will, in
most cases, be functionally illiterate. The streets may be filled
with armies of policemen, but violent crime and civil disorder
will decrease very little. If, however, the lower class were to
disappear—if, say, its members were overnight to acquire the
attitudes, motivations, and habits of the working class—the
most serious and intractable problems of the city would disappear with it. . . . [14]

Believing that if the world's poor would develop new values,
prosperity would follow, David Chilton has satirized Ron Sider's
Rich Christians in an Age of Hunger: "In Sider's social theory,
everyone is miserable: if you're poor, the rich oppress you, and if
you're rich, God overthrows you. Sort of like Cosmic Hot-Potato—
up, down, up, down, up, down; the last one with the money goes
to hell. . . ."[15] So, with tongue in cheek, Chilton recommends that
we "construct a new economics, an economics of 'compassion for
the poor,' an economics of the Tender-Hearted Elimination of Free
Trade (THEFT)."[16]

Work habits in the industrialized world do seem to require
certain values—efficiency, schedule consciousness, goal orientation, et cetera. Individuals, groups, and nations that want to mod-
ernize must make value choices. They must choose, for example,
between capital accumulation and the expected redistribution of
profits among kin. Yet in Chapters Four and Five we have explored
ways to honor ties with kin while cultivating modern business
habits. And, while certain values may be conducive to economic
growth, our American amalgam of values is not the only efficient
one.

In light of Banfield's argument that "new attitudes" would
solve the cities' most serious problems, we must not forget the
power of repressive structures. "'It is naive to affirm that all that is
needed is new men in order to have a new society,'" said Samuel
Escobar recently. "'Certainly every man should do whatever he is
able to do to get the transforming message of Christ to his fellow
citizens. But it is also true that it is precisely these new men who
sometimes need to transform the structures of society so that

there may be less injustice, less opportunity for man to do evil to man, for exploitation.'"[17]

Both changes in local values and international political and economic changes are part of development. While unjust distribution systems are powerful, helping people produce more crops and goods amounts to something. In this book it is argued that agricultural aid harms a person without land. That may not be strictly true. Recent research indicates that urban squatters can grow most of the vegetables they need in containers that take up just a few square feet—without owning an inch of land!

No single approach is "the answer." We need a comprehensive view of the world and its needs. Jon and Ariel take these kinds of criteria into consideration when they share their resources.

"Of course it's work," they admit, as they reflect on how their priorities contrast with those of many of their Christian friends. "For most of us, the 'simple lifestyle' is not simple. Especially at first, it takes work and planning."

Yet Jon and Ariel feel rich—not only because of their physical resources, but also because they have the privilege of participating actively in the battle for Christ's kingdom. In a decade when suicide among affluent American youth has jumped 250 percent, Jon and Ariel suffer from no such narcissistic ennui. Yet they are not disciplining their spending for some will-o'-the-wisp idea of the counterculture, but rather for a key individual in a specific community. His project is not just saving people to starve; it is integrated holistic development. It is not just modernizing the community technically; it is also raising Haitians' consciousness of the causes of their poverty, and of what they can do to transform these structures. It is freeing them spiritually and socially.

Jon and Ariel feel they are part of God's foreign policy. That's richness.

---

1. Eugene Peterson, *A Long Obedience in the Same Direction* (Downers Grove, Ill.: Inter-Varsity Press, 1980), p. 11.

2. Darien Cooper, *You Can Be the Wife of a Happy Husband* (Wheaton, Ill.: Victor Books, 1974), p. 51.

3. Catherine Bramwell-Booth, *Catherine Booth* (London: Hodder and Stoughton, 1970).

4. Karen Mains, *Open Heart, Open Home* (Elgin, Ill.: David C. Cook Publishing Co., 1976).

5. Kari Torjesen Malcolm, *Women at the Crossroads* (Downers Grove, Ill.: Inter-Varsity Press, 1982), pp. 35, 42.

6. John Alexander, "Kingdom World," *The Other Side,* Aug. 1979, p. 12.

7. William Krutza, "The Near-Sighted Ethics of Christian Businessmen," *Eternity,* Sept. 1976, pp. 15-17, 40.

8. James Buchan, *The Expendable Mary Slessor* (New York: Seabury Press, 1981).

9. Interview with Tim LaHaye, *The Wittenburg Door,* June-July 1980, p. 12.

10. John Brobeck, "Why Am I Unhappy as a Professional Scientist?" *Wheaton Alumni Magazine,* April 1975, p. 4.

11. *Ibid.*

12. Quoted in Cynthia Schaible's "The Gospel of the Good Life," *Eternity,* Feb. 1981, p. 26.

13. Interview with Richard DeVos, *Eternity,* Feb. 1981, p. 23.

14. Edward C. Banfield, *The Unheavenly City Revisited* (Boston: Little, Brown, 1974), p. 234.

15. David Chilton, *Productive Christians in an Age of Guilt Manipulators: A Biblical Response to Ron Sider* (Tyler, Tex.: Institute for Christian Economics, 1981), p. 69.

16. *Ibid.,* p. 86.

17. Samuel Escobar, quoted in *Campus Impact,* the magazine of the Philippine Inter-Varsity Christian Fellowship, Sept. 1982, p. 5.

Printed in the United States
42972LVS00004B/144